About the author

Dr Gian Luca Gardini is Lecturer in International Relations and Latin American Politics at the University of Bath. His works have been published in the UK, Europe, the United States and South America. His most recent books are *The Origins of Mercosur* and, together with Dr P. W. Lambert, *Latin American Foreign Policies between Ideology and Pragmatism*. Dr Gardini has also acted as a practitioner of international and EU affairs: he was Representative to the EU of the Italian Confederation of Industry, and International Trade Adviser to Eurochambres, the European Association of Chambers of Commerce and Industry.

LATIN AMERICA IN THE 21ST CENTURY

nations, regionalism, globalization

Gian Luca Gardini

translated by Gemma Brown

Zed Books
LONDON | NEW YORK

Latin America in the 21st Century: Nations, Regionalism, Globalization was first published in English in 2012 by Zed Books Ltd, 7 Cynthia Street, London N1 9JF, UK and Room 400, 175 Fifth Avenue, New York, NY 10010, USA

Originally published in Italian in 2009 under the title *L'America Latina nel XXI secolo* by Carocci Editore S.p.A., Via Sardegna 50, 00187 Roma, Italia

www.zedbooks.co.uk

Set in Monotype Sabon and Gill Sans Heavy by Ewan Smith, London
Index: ed.emery@thefreeuniversity.net
Cover designed by Rogue Four Design
Cover photo © Getty Images/Tom Till
Printed and bound by CPI Group (UK) Ltd, Croydon, CR0 4YY

Distributed in the USA exclusively by Palgrave Macmillan, a division of St Martin's Press, LLC, 175 Fifth Avenue, New York, NY 10010, USA

A catalogue record for this book is available from the British Library
Library of Congress Cataloging in Publication Data available

ISBN 978 1 78032 089 2 hb
ISBN 978 1 78032 088 5 pb

Contents

For my parents

Introduction

Latin America is a vast, diverse and marvellous continent, rich in history, culture, and political and social experimentation. It is also, along with the wider world, going through a phase of transition. Categories and concepts that have traditionally been employed to study the continent, such as underdevelopment, poverty, dependency, left and right, East and West, no longer capture appropriately the complexity and evolution of present-day Latin America. They need to be discussed and redefined in the light of the new context and challenges of our times. There is hardly an unequivocal definition or uncontested notion of what Latin America is today.

The very concept of Latin America itself is under strain. Mexico, Central America and the Caribbean increasingly gravitate to the orbit of the United States. Conversely South America seems to be distancing itself from the North and emerging as a region of its own, with giant Brazil offering a kind of ambiguous leadership to this project. But even this shift is far from uncontested, steady or irreversible. Latin America remains a resilient, although heterogeneous, cultural and political concept as well as a useful analytical category.

The reading of twenty-first-century Latin America that this book proposes is one of nuances and dilemmas rather than one of established interpretations and linear trajectories. The book is structured according to three levels of discussion: the states, the region, and Latin America in the world. Some of the issues discussed are peculiar to one nation or a group of countries. There are other significant features that broadly characterize the Latin American region as a whole or subregions within it. Finally there are developments in the international relations of Latin America and the place it occupies on the world stage. At each level twenty-first-century Latin America displays, and often struggles with, three major tensions.

First, there is a tension between rhetoric and pragmatism, or more widely between ideology and pragmatism. These are not incompatible and a surge in both has recently taken place. This is particularly evident at the level of individual states and administrations in Latin America. This tension partly explains the coexistence of apparently divergent, if not contradictory, political and economic choices and stances, such as the strongly anti-US rhetoric of Venezuelan president Hugo Chávez and the close commercial links between the two countries, or the combination of former president Lula of Brazil's strong social commitment and his extremely orthodox and conservative economic policy. In the first decade of the twenty-first century, a period of transition, the quest for new ideals, recipes, flexibility and adaptability in fact reveals a pragmatic approach to the situation rather than fundamental incoherence.

A wholesale rejection of globalization or isolation from its effects would be impossible: there is too much interdependence in the areas of politics, economics, society, the environment and culture. What is possible, however, is the combination of economic openness and social policies, a 'good neighbour' foreign policy and national interests and cultural identity, and sustainable economic development and local needs. The lively and deeply ideological rhetoric which has always been a characteristic of Latin American politics seems, at this juncture in history, to blend well with rediscovered pragmatism. On the one hand, the rhetorical emphasis helps to draw attention to certain issues and, possibly, to reach pragmatic results. On the other hand, pragmatism allows for the negotiation of solutions with fundamentally ideological aims. Rhetoric is not an end in itself, but it does serve specific national interests. Pragmatism highlights the limits and restrictions which exponents of an excessively ideological approach could face in an increasingly interconnected and interdependent world, characterized by a plethora of actors, interests and issues on the agenda, domestically, regionally and internationally.

Secondly, a tension between unity and diversity is plainly visible. Latin America is often considered a single entity, but its diversity is at least as great as that of the European continent. The differences between a Chilean and a Colombian are just as obvious and profound as those between a Finn and a Spaniard. Even within the same country, highly varying economic, social and cultural realities can be found. For example, Brazil is home to both a south which closely resembles Europe and the proudly black African Bahia region; both the skyscrapers and financial quarters of São Paulo and the extreme poverty and backwardness of some areas in the north-east. The concept of Latin America is elusive and heterogeneous not only culturally, but also in terms of its geography. The definition 'Latin', for instance, does not cover indigenous populations. French-speaking Quebec in Canada is not associated with the Latin part of the continent, while English-speaking Belize or Dutch-speaking Caribbean islands are generally included in the definition. Nonetheless, 'Latin America' is a universally accepted term and Latin Americans are proud to call themselves '*nosotros los latinos*'. Above all, the 'Latin' part of the Americas stands as a counterpoint to its 'other', namely North America: the United States and Canada. It is perhaps little wonder that this variety translates into a wealth of differing mindsets, histories and ideas between and within nations.

Despite their differences, Latin American countries share a number of traits. No single country is yet fully part of the so-called industrialized world, despite advances in Brazil rapidly moving the country towards achieving world power status. Latin American countries have long been, and for the most part remain, highly dependent on global markets, especially in the domains of raw materials and foodstuffs. They all fall to a larger or lesser extent under the sphere of influence of the United States, a country which has played a fundamental role in their history. What's more, all of these countries have roots in Western civilization:[1] the *conquistadores* managed to impose not only their political regime but also their language, religion and values. Finally, Latin American countries share a similar social structure, with a focus on landownership, a unique form of modernization characterized by delayed but accelerated industrialization, and socio-economic disparity. These remarks provide a snapshot of the tensions between unity and diversity in twenty-first-century Latin America. This is epitomized by the number of regional integration projects purportedly pursuing continental unity. Their variety in membership, rationale, and political and economic proposals is in fact a stark reflection of diversity and heterogeneity.

Thirdly, there is a tension between change and continuity, often resulting in a symbiosis of highly ambitious political, economic and social experimentation and structural limitations. In recent years, the aftermath of the Cold War and the 1990s neoliberal model have laid the foundations for events which have defined, for better or for worse, the Latin America of the new millennium. It would be impossible, and perhaps undesirable, to sweep this inheritance under the carpet. The end of the Cold War signalled the victory of the Western model based on democracy and free trade. However, the adoption of the neoliberal paradigm, based on these principles, has fallen short of resolving two age-old problems: the organization of the democratic state and its approach to development. Quality of democracy in many Latin American countries is somewhat low, while the neoliberal economic model has failed to solve the riddles of modernization and economic and social inequality. Thus associations have been formed in the Latin American mindset between neoliberalism and inequality, poverty and external pressure, giving rise to a motley mixture of desires for reform, reactions to the past and national autonomy.

These reactions have assumed highly diverse forms which are sometimes radical in nature. Crucially, there is no unequivocal approach to the total or partial changes in pre-existing economic models and state organization. The result is a clear tension between change and continuity. On the one hand, there are structural elements both internationally and nationally which remain almost unchanged, such as the asymmetrical balance of power between Latin American countries and the United States, Latin America's economic interdependence with export markets, and the unequal distribution of wealth and national resources. On the other hand there are newer elements, such as the emergence of extra-continental powers and alliances as alternatives to the United States, including the European Union and more recently China, the adoption of new economic models which seek to move on from neoliberal precepts with varying degrees of criticism, and a generation of progressive leaders with new ideas who want to find internal solutions to the problems of the continent. The tension between change and continuity is particularly apparent in the international relations of Latin America.

The book is divided thematically and articulated from the specific to the general. Chapter 1 analyses individual nation-states. Chapter 2 focuses on Latin American regionalism and the various projects of regional integration, while Chapter 3 discusses Latin America's place on the global stage. Whereas the tensions between rhetoric and pragmatism, unity and diversity, and change and continuity are present in all three areas, one specific tension is most pertinent to each sector. The tension between rhetoric and pragmatism is best embodied at the national level, that between unity and diversity at the regional level, and that between change and continuity at the global level. The combination of these tensions and themes is the key both to reading the following pages and to understanding Latin America in the twenty-first century.

ONE

The states of Latin America: between rhetoric and pragmatism

Introduction

The most eye-catching state-level phenomenon following the dawn of the new millennium in Latin America has probably been the rise of governments generally identified as socialist and progressive, which prioritize a social agenda. The electoral earthquake which has rocked Latin America during the past decade, casting out stalwart proponents of 1990s neoliberalism in favour of those with a distinct social and populist rhetoric, began in 1998 with the election of Hugo Chávez in Venezuela and continued until 2011 with Ollanta Humala's victory in Peru. This phenomenon, bringing left-leaning parties and candidates into government, was dubbed the 'pink tide'. This colour signals a stark difference from the traditional Latin American socialist parties of the 1960s and 1970s, deeply ideological movements linked in various ways and in varying degrees to Marxism-Leninism, which could thus be defined as 'red'. In spite of their common progressive intentions and commitment to fighting social inequality in their respective countries, leaders such as Lula in Brazil, the Kirchners in Argentina or Bachelet in Chile share no clear common ideology, certainly not a Marxist one. Instead, their progressive and nationalist rhetoric is mixed with wide-ranging pragmatism in both internal and – usually – international affairs. Their imprint, perhaps most accurately described as broadly social-democratic, has brought the left in contemporary Latin America closer to a pink colouring.

Nonetheless, this wave is much less unusual and, significantly, less homogeneous than at first sight. This wave of ideological conformism, if it can be called such – and there are serious doubts in this regard – is not unprecedented in nature or in breadth. The neoliberal era of the 1980s and 1990s probably had a stronger and, it appears at present, longer-lasting practical impact than the pink tide. The diffusion of neoliberal ideology and economic policies in Latin America was much deeper, wider and more homogeneous than the pink tide. Following the collapse of the Soviet Union and the triumph of the Western democratic political model and market economy, all Latin American countries (and others besides) wholeheartedly and consistently embraced the neoliberal doctrine. In the second half of the 1990s all of the countries in Latin America with the exception of Cuba had neoliberal governments. The crisis of this same model and its inability to solve the long-standing problems of Latin American underdevelopment, including grave social inequality, sparked counter-reactions in the form of total rejection (Chávez) or adaptation and evolution (Lula and Bachelet).

The pink tide is therefore neither homogeneous nor linear.[1] It is neither a hard-and-fast phenomenon nor a consistent turn to the left. Rather than the simplified version of facts portrayed by mass media, we are in fact dealing with several complex political phenomena, each shaped by different historical, political and economic factors specific to the respective countries. At times, the actors and parties grouped under the collective umbrella of the 'pink tide' are worlds apart. Furthermore, there remain a number of governments in Latin America which can be defined as centre-right (such as those in Mexico, Colombia and certain Central American countries), and in reality many of the so-called 'pink' governments employ economic policies which are not dissimilar from those of neoliberalism (Lula in Brazil, Kirchner in Argentina and Bachelet in Chile). In political practices, there are striking differences among these perceived 'pink tide' administrations. These differences span from the concept of the state and its role in the economy, to policies promoting democracy, good governance and transparency, to the breadth and nature of involvement in social affairs and foreign policy positions. Finally, there are the sometimes considerable differences between practice and rhetoric, between what leaders say they want to do and what they actually do, and between good intentions and the structural limitations of the domestic and international landscapes.

This chapter specifically examines five case studies: Brazil,

Argentina, Chile, Venezuela and Bolivia. These cases are essential for an understanding of the dynamics of contemporary Latin America. This is followed by an overview of the rest of Latin America in order to provide a comprehensive portrayal of the problems and proposed solutions and to assess the impact of the pink tide upon the present and future of the continent. The analysis covers the past twenty to thirty years, a sufficiently extended period to contextualize situations historically without losing emphasis on the transition from the 1990s neoliberal model to the counter-reaction of the twenty-first century.

Brazil

Brazil has the largest territory and population of all Latin American countries. It has often been taken as a point of reference politically and culturally by other nations in the area but has been reluctant to take a clear regional leadership role so far. Brazil has long had reason to expect a glorious future. The country has considerable assets, including mineral deposits, an abundant oil supply, fertile soil where practically anything can be cultivated, rich biodiversity and enviable woodland and fresh water resources. Recent offshore oil discoveries may soon convert Brazil into a major oil-exporting country. However, it also has considerable problems: widespread poverty, one of the worst inequality indexes in the world, high crime rates, malnutrition and poor levels of education, limitations on democracy and corruption. These weaknesses have all kept the 'country of the future' out of reach for almost two hundred years since its independence. Now, the future could be close at hand, and Brazil is preparing to become a world power, at least at the economic level.

After around twenty years of dictatorship, Brazil returned to democracy in 1985 and can now claim to be a stable democratic regime. In comparison to the other military governments of South America, the Brazilian dictatorship was relatively mild, with a much cleaner record on violence and human rights abuse than those of nearby Chile or Argentina. In addition, the military regime attempted to uphold a semblance of legality and institutional legitimacy, and left behind an industrial structure and culture which were unparalleled in the rest of Latin America. Whether or not the price to pay in terms of foreign debt and civil and social repression was just or acceptable is another question. Yet despite these relative advantages in comparison to other countries, democracy was not established easily.

The first democratic administration (1985–90), led by President Sarney, was characterized by both political and economic instability. Its main priorities were consolidating democracy and fighting inflation, a deep-seated problem in Brazil which continued to stunt economic growth. A new democratic constitution was approved in 1988, but unfortunately contained elements which would hinder the control of public debt and the democratic governability of the country. In the economic domain, Sarney introduced a stabilization plan which brought in a new currency and froze prices, wages and exchange rates. The short-term results were superb, but the inflexibility of this plan and the government's inability to adapt it over time led to economic overheating. After a couple of years the economy was in an even worse state than before. Towards the end of Sarney's mandate inflation passed the 1,000 per cent threshold and poor economic growth combined with deep, enduring social divisions triggered a major crisis.[2] This had a negative impact on the economy and caused a worrying fragmentation of political parties. Although the democratic regime maintained a fair record in terms of legitimacy and popular support for its first attempt, the same cannot be said for the progress made in the economic and social sectors.

In 1990 a young and relatively unknown governor from a backwater state in the poor north-east was sworn in as head of state. Fernando Collor de Mello was able to exploit influential friendships, media power, political fragmentation and the fears of international investors as well as the domestic entrepreneurial establishment in São Paulo, the economic heart of the country, regarding the Workers' Party (Partido dos Trabalhadores, PT) candidate. This was trade unionist Luiz Inácio Lula da Silva, at that time a left-wing radical. The Collor experiment was overall unsuccessful, not so much for its policies as for the scandals which dogged the president. Collor began the necessary task of opening up and cleaning out the economy by instigating a process of privatization, reducing trade barriers and trying to whittle down the exorbitant numbers of civil servants. He had notable successes in foreign policy, including the signature of the regional integration agreement Mercosur along with Argentina, Paraguay and Uruguay, and an agreement with Argentina on the use of nuclear energy for peaceful means. Both Collor himself and the cautious reforms he tried to introduce were, however, destroyed by a series of corruption scandals which ended with the Brazilian Congress declaring the president's impeachment. Brazilian democracy proved its worth once again by removing the president from office, but the country's grave economic and social problems remained unresolved.

The neoliberal reforms which Collor had introduced in Brazil were actually brought to completion by President Fernando Henrique Cardoso, an internationally renowned sociologist of Marxist origins, who had entered politics. Collor's empty presidential seat was initially occupied by his vice-president, Itamar Franco, who will probably be best remembered for appointing Cardoso as finance minister. In this role, Cardoso adopted the most efficient macroeconomic stabilization plan in the history of Brazil: the *Plano Real*. Shock measures were ruled out, a balanced budget law was drawn up and a unit of account was introduced in advance of the adoption of a stronger, more stable currency, named the real. The process was similar to the creation of the ECU as precursor to the euro in order to stabilize prices and familiarize economic operators with the value of the new currency. These measures, along with deliberately high interest and exchange rates, proved successful. Inflation dropped from 929 per cent in 1993 to 4 per cent in 1997.[3] Such success propelled Cardoso into the presidency, where PT candidate Lula was once again defeated.

Cardoso's two mandates (1994–98 and 1998–2002) marked a decisive swing towards economic openness and modernization and the adoption of neoliberal measures. Initially the potential costs in terms of unemployment and reduced public spending, including on welfare, were considered temporary necessities. National and international approval for the kind of economic policy choices recommended by Cardoso was almost unanimous. Although results were positive in many areas, they did not live up to expectations, leaving the country's persistent problems of poverty and inequality largely unsolved. Cardoso implemented an extremely prudent economic policy to consolidate macroeconomic stability, but this did not produce sufficiently high growth rates to generate resources for development. A broad privatization process was rolled out and public spending was cut significantly, but adverse international conditions (the crises in Asia in 1997, Russia in 1998 and Argentina in 2001) and mounting internal opposition choked the government's reformist ambitions.

Despite some positive results in the fight against poverty and the improvement of the population's living conditions, social policy was neither a priority nor a possibility for Cardoso's government given the scarcity of resources. The government's legacy was a stable economy and increasing credibility on the international scene. However, these were coupled with a series of ongoing problems in health, education, agrarian reform, the protection and development of the Amazon area and, ironically, economic growth, which had remained low and failed to generate the necessary resources for social progress. The ground was laid for a more ambitious and radical president; someone who would place social issues at the top of the political agenda, speak on behalf of the millions of marginalized Brazilians in the poor countryside and deprived urban districts, and tackle head-on the problems of poverty and inequality which continued to corrode Brazilian society.

Like Allende in Chile or Mitterrand in France, Lula won the elections on his fourth attempt to become the first 'working-class' president in the nation's history in 2003. His reputation as working-class president or president of the poor had perhaps more to do with his exploits as a young man than his action in government. Born into a very modest family with two illiterate parents, Lula himself had only a limited education. He had first-hand experience of rural poverty, migration into urban areas, factory work and trade union involvement. He stood out among the founders of the Workers' Party in 1980 and later on for his radically hostile stance on the Cardoso administration's privatizations and attempts to modernize the economy.

Lula's candidacy in 2002 had once again aroused fears in economic and financial sectors as well as, to some extent, among the middle class, even though most Brazilian voters were now convinced that the only way to encourage development, reduce crime and become a major international player was to face up to the country's grave social problems. Both Lula and the Workers' Party recognized that in order first to be elected and then to govern the country, they needed to win the votes and trust of the middle classes and, just as importantly, the moneyed classes. Thus they adopted a moderate image, adopting a socio-democratic model along European lines, sidelining their most radical demands and actually pledging to continue the harsh economic policies instigated by Cardoso, but without abandoning the social agenda. This strategy of combining ideology with pragmatism, hyperbolic rhetoric with moderated action, paid off and Lula was elected with over 60 per cent of votes in the second round. Most of the votes came from the rich and developed southern states.

Evaluations and appraisals of Lula's two mandates include areas of light and shade. But considering the enormity of Brazil's problems, there are reasons for satisfaction and optimism. Indeed, he left the presidency in 2010 with an impressive approval rate of about 80 per cent. After shelving their radical rhetoric and proposals for unachievable reforms, the Lula government obtained significant political, economic and social results, even in the midst of scandal and difficulty. In the political sphere, Lula managed to build up his pool of electoral consensus, including in the poorest north-eastern regions, without alienating support (or perhaps neutrality) from the business sector, particularly in the state of São Paulo, the economic heart of the country. Increased parliamentary support, achieved by enlarging the coalition, paved the way for significant reforms and allowed Lula to overcome corruption scandals which, although not directly involving the president, had weakened the PT. In economic terms Brazil has been in fine shape during the past few years: it was robust enough to survive the global economic and financial crisis of late 2008 and it has in fact emerged from it quickly and with a booming economy. The continuation of Cardoso's policies has proved fruitful. Although growth has remained relatively slow compared to that of other neighbouring or emerging countries, the indicators are all positive. Relationships with international financial organizations are good, foreign debt is being repaid at a steady rate and both the export market and the attraction of foreign investors have made huge advances.

After some initial setbacks, social policy, the much-vaunted flagship principle of the Lula administration, is now producing good results. Ditching an ineffective propaganda-based strategy for directly supplying families with food (the *Projeto Fome Zero* or Zero Hunger Programme, a real headache for the government in its first two years), focus switched to a conditional cash transfer system for families. Put more simply, the government pays benefits to families that commit to sending their children to school and for medical check-ups (the *Bolsa Familia* programme). This is an efficient method for fighting child labour and juvenile delinquency, improving school attendance rates, health and the possibility of future employment, and helping lower-income families directly and practically. This strategy has had an immediate impact, but its best results may yet lie in the medium- or long-term future: better-educated and looked-after children will enjoy higher salaries and better health conditions as adults. In turn, with high wages they will pay high taxes and with good health they will not be a burden on the social system, thus increasing public resources available for further development projects and generating a virtuous circle.

The combination of macroeconomic policies targeting long-term stability and sustainable economic growth and effective and truly redistributive social policies has yielded a record result: inequality started decreasing for the first time in Brazilian history, and according to data published by the Getulio Vargas Foundation, most Brazilians are now no longer members of the lowest social stratum but part of the middle class, a remarkable advancement.[4] What's more, the expansion of the middle class has absorbed some of both the poorest and richest sectors of the population, thus shrinking the inequality gap. This is even more amazing when one considers the long time period required to alter this kind of semi-structural feature of a society. Of course, there is still a lot to do, and these results are not a point of arrival but of departure. Still, the achievements of the Lula administration confirm that good policies and good administrators and leaders do make a difference.

Many problems nonetheless remain on Brazil's agenda. Faster economic growth is needed; however, the main problem is in fact the innate contradiction of an essentially export-based development model. First, international prices for Brazil's main exports, foodstuffs and minerals, are currently sky high, but how will growth and development be sustained if these prices fall? Secondly, and more importantly, Brazil's growth is built on exports and the real's relatively low exchange rate. With the export boom and increases in foreign direct investment and currency reserves, the real will gain in value compared to the currencies of the principal import countries for Brazilian goods – indeed, a comparison of the dollar and the real shows that this process has already begun. Consequently, Brazilian goods will become more expensive on international markets and the sector could witness a downturn. As a result the whole economy, highly dependent on the export sector, could suffer. Industry in particular could bear the brunt, as it has fewer comparative advantages (in terms of labour costs and technology) and is also a major employer. Finally the 2008 global crisis, by reducing purchasing power and therefore demand in traditional Brazilian export markets, could lead to a slowdown of both economic and social development in Brazil. So far this shift has been more than compensated by the surge in demand from China and other Asian countries. Such a dependency on export markets, however, may have a downside too.

There are just as many challenges in the political and social domains. Corruption remains commonplace both at federal and state levels, and political fragmentation makes the country difficult to govern. With regard to society, the number of poor and people on the margins remains extremely high. Alarming crime levels, widespread unemployment, agrarian reform and rural living conditions as well as the stewardship of the Amazon all call for immediate action. In spite of these multiple liabilities, Brazil seems to be on the right track, an observation confirmed by its improved international clout along with its ability to influence the global agenda and act as a catalyst for the developing world. The award of the football World Cup in 2014 and the Olympic Games in 2016 is testament to the feel-good mood that currently pervades the country and informs its image abroad.

However, becoming a world power is a complicated process and involves choices of image, identity and substance: is Brazil an advanced or a developing country? Do its vital interests more closely resemble those of the North or the South? Thus far Brazil has managed to keep a foot in both camps and smooth over apparent contradictions, but there is one fundamental trait of a superpower that Brazil has already: the true drivers of its foreign policy are national interest and economic growth. 'Third World' solidarity, both in rhetoric and, more significantly, in practice, is referred to only when convenient. In its bid for a permanent seat on the UN Security Council, Brazil has acquired more support from countries with similar ambitions (India and South Africa) than from the rest of the Latin American continent. As the designated regional leader, it is not in Brazil's interest to allow its own international advancement to be hindered by its neighbours. These neighbours could be useful if they add regional weight to Brazil's international positions, but if not, Brazil is capable of striking out alone, as revealed by recent events in the World Trade Organization (WTO) and relations with the USA. In reality, Brazil is often closer to Washington than to the developing world in international forums:[5] consider their agenda on security, drug trafficking, terrorism, money laundering, industrial and, often, commercial policy. As a world leader Brazil could benefit the whole of Latin America, as long as Brasilia shoulders the burdens as well as the blessings of such a position. If not, Brazil would simply mirror the current relationship between Latin America and the United States. Lula's administration has been characterized by a cunning blend of ideology and pragmatism in internal policy, and this is now being rolled out internationally. It is now for newly elected president Dilma Rousseff, the first woman to hold the highest post in the nation, to manage the legacy of Lula. Also a PT leader and massively sponsored by Lula himself, Dilma has promised continuity with her predecessor and her first 100 days in power have substantially confirmed this line: the medium- and long-term developments and consequences have yet to be seen.

Argentina

Argentina, like Brazil, is also blessed with fine resources above and below ground. It has fertile land, abundant water resources and can also boast comparatively high levels of education and a generally well-qualified workforce. Unlike Brazil, however, Argentina is not the country of the future but one of the past. The world's eighth-biggest economy in the early 1900s, it was a politically and culturally advanced country nurturing a close relationship with Europe, a continent with which it identified in many ways. With the end of the agricultural export model, the rise of mass politics and Europe's waning influence on the world scene in the interwar years, Argentina sank into an inexorable decline, progressively losing momentum, competitiveness and economic, political and cultural importance. Nostalgia for the past and a misplaced sense of grandeur have often prevented Argentina from examining its problems cogently, often leading to short-term plans and inconsistency in political and economic choices. Between the 1950s and 1980s, and especially as a legacy of the Perón experience and the military administrations, this generated a great deal of the political, economic and social ills which the country is struggling even now to shake off. These problems include state deficit, foreign debt, patronage and favours in politics, macroeconomic instability and a general lack of vision, often associated with a crisis of identity, divided between the chimera of Europe and the reality of Latin America.

With the fall of the military dictatorship (1976–83), Raúl Alfonsín of the Radical Civic Union (Unión Cívica Radical, UCR) became president of the new democracy. His priorities were democratic consolidation, economic recovery and pursuing the military responsible for inflicting torture and violence during the dictatorship. The last objective met with strong resistance from the military and other sectors that had benefited from their rule and had to be quickly abandoned. With annual inflation close to 1,000 per cent and foreign debt of around $45 billion, the economy was in dire straits.[6] A stabilization plan was adopted which froze prices and wages for an indefinite period and cut public spending. However, these measures conflicted with the aim of democratic consolidation. Resistance from the population, the state apparatus and the provinces threatened the social and political stability of a still-fragile system, so these provisions had to be reversed. This exposed the dilemma between addressing the needs of economic austerity and confronting social pressures. Plumping for the second option, public spending began to increase again, annual inflation returned to over 1,000 per cent, foreign debt rose to $62 billion in 1989 and the economy went into recession.[7] Argentina began to become convinced that drastic measures were required to tackle this profound crisis.

Carlos Menem of the Peronist party (Partido Justicialista, PJ) won the 1989 elections, promising an industrial revolution based on traditional Peronist principles such as wage increases and support for national industry. Initially the economic measures did not deliver the desired growth, and a series of amnesties and pardons for the military dented Menem's popularity. The turning point came during late 1990 and early 1991. Leaving aside Peronist traditions of strong state intervention and expansive economic policies, Menem converted to neoliberalism, implementing a swift and drastic reduction in the role of the state, the privatization of major public industries, economic openness, export-based development and deregulation of production activities. The finance minister, Domingo Cavallo, introduced the so-called 'convertibility' plan, replacing the national currency, the *austral*, with the new peso, which was given a fixed exchange rate of 1:1 with the US dollar. The *Convertibilidad* plan achieved remarkable results in reducing inflation, which fell to single figures within a few weeks.

In spite of this, Menem's management of the economy did not resolve any of the grave Argentine structural deficiencies. Instead, it created a false illusion of stability and prosperity, replacing some of the most pressing problems with others which in all probability triggered the devastating crisis in 2001. A wide-scale privatization process was carried out in such diverse sectors as oil, gas, air and rail transport, water, electricity, telephones and the health system. This produced a rapid, copious influx of foreign capital, which on the one hand disguised the serious problems of insufficient tax revenue and staggering amounts of public debt and on the other led to widespread unemployment caused by the restructuring of companies and deprived the country of its manufacturing infrastructure in key sectors, leaving this instead in foreign hands. In the absence of sufficient tax collection and limits on public spending, especially in the federal provinces, the only way to finance the convertibility model was through loans from international markets, which further swelled foreign debt.

Towards the end of the Menem administration's second mandate, the economy went into recession and corruption scandals stemming chiefly from privatizations drove voters to dismiss Peronism in favour of the *Alianza*. This was a coalition of the UCR and the Frente País Solidario (FREPASO), a social-democratic group which proposed a blend of free trade and social reformism. However, the new president, Fernando de la Rúa, had made a serious error of judgement, believing he had inherited a stable and consolidated economy and development model which just needed a few tweaks in competitiveness and, especially, social affairs. This was quite simply not the case. Foreign debt had more than doubled since 1990, hovering at the $130–140 billion mark, and the public deficit had become untenable.[8] The Menemist economic model had enriched a tiny minority but impoverished the majority of the nation. Unemployment reached 20 per cent in 2001, and some sources estimate that over 50 per cent of the population were living below the poverty threshold.[9] The privatization process turned out to be largely inefficient and the rigidity of the convertibility system meant that the exchange rate could not be used to relaunch the economy or control the balance of payments. The economic survival of the state, now almost unable to pay civil servants' wages, was dependent on emergency loans from the International Monetary Fund.

Lumbered with paying back the debts of the previous administration, de la Rúa had to abandon his electoral campaign promises and resolutions and resort to emergency measures. However, the government found itself faced with harsh and diffuse criticism. The newly mobilized unemployed now thronged the streets to picket, driving a social protest which could neither be appeased nor repressed. The Peronist opposition, which had won control of Congress, blocked any significant attempt to reduce public spending and made it practically impossible to cut social services dispensed through the trade unions or limit spending by the provinces. International investors exacerbated the situation: their endorsement of austerity and stabilization conflicted with the needs of a state in crisis, eager to restart the economy and avoid further contraction of spending and investment. The weakness and internal divisions of the government coalition and the president's indecision worsened the situation still further.

Domingo Cavallo, the inventor of convertibility, was reappointed to steer the economy and given considerable powers. He unilaterally increased tariff barriers to stimulate domestic production, irritating commercial partners, particularly Brazil, Argentina's major partner and key associate in the regional integration project Mercosur. Cavallo was also seeking a way to bring convertibility to an end. However, this would have caused grave social repercussions by dramatically and suddenly reducing the value of savings and investments, and would have alarmed international creditors. With no other alternative, Cavallo tried to renegotiate foreign debt by exchanging short-term bonds, whose interest rates Argentina could not honour, for long-term bonds with even higher interest rates. This triggered a capital flight from the country which almost toppled the entire banking system. Cavallo set strict limits on withdrawals and movement of capital, freezing access to bank accounts and savings for millions of citizens. This measure, known as the *corralito*, marked the end of convertibility as well as the de la Rúa government among a wave of street protests and social unrest.

In December 2001 street protests descended into mayhem: supermarkets were ransacked and country-wide demonstrations took place. With public order on the brink of collapse and the presidential palace surrounded by the mob, de la Rúa left office, escaping by helicopter. The power vacuum lasted for about two weeks before Eduardo Duhalde, the Peronist party leader of the Buenos Aires province, was appointed to preside over the transition phase until the mandate of the resigning de la Rúa expired. In the meantime, Argentina had defaulted on its loans, meaning it was unable to repay them, and the peso had fallen in value to 3.5:1 against the dollar. Duhalde avoided any decisions which might have added fuel to the fire and managed to safeguard legitimate democracy (a commendable result in itself given the severity of the crisis), pacifying the protest and even achieving slight economic recovery in the run-up to elections. These turned out to be a turning point in Argentina's recent history.

The 2003 elections were unusual to say the least, but they resulted in government measures and economic achievements which surpassed even the most optimistic predictions. With the traditional political parties discredited and fragmented, no strong candidates emerged. Feelings of resignation and lack of trust within the country reached record levels. A popular slogan was '*que se vayan todos*' (all go home), which signalled a profound crisis of credibility of all public institutions. Although no candidate achieved a majority in the first round, the former president, Carlos Menem, sensationally scooped the most votes (24 per cent), followed by Néstor Kirchner, another Peronist and governor of the remote Patagonian province of Santa Cruz. In a move which may be unique in history, Menem decided to withdraw from the campaign. Polls suggested he would lose by over forty points in the ensuing ballot. Mounting protest against him and international scepticism towards the prospect of his re-election were the last straw. Néstor Kirchner, a relatively unknown politician in national circles, was elected without a vote in the second round after winning just 22 per cent of support in the first. This was a shaky start for the new administration, and few would have bet on its performance or endurance.

Without rejecting the foundations of modern capitalism, Kirchner adopted a pragmatic economic policy, combining state and market, resisting pressure from the International Monetary Fund to implement structural adjustments and instead prioritizing industrial recovery and employment. A flexible exchange rate was adopted which favoured exports, reindustrialization policies were brought in and considerable fiscal and commercial gains were recouped. Between 2002 and 2006, Argentina grew at a stable annual rate of over 8 per cent[10] (and after a temporary slowdown due to the international financial crisis GDP grew by 8.2 per cent in 2010[11]). Foreign debts were vigorously renegotiated and significant concessions were acquired on most of the country's bonds. Although these measures were badly received by international investors and small-time savers, the Argentine government's actions reduced the burden of debt drastically and sufficiently to generate resources for development.[12] Kirchner also demonstrated his unwillingness to rely on the International Monetary Fund by repaying all of Argentina's debt to this institution in one lump sum. This move also had a strong impact in terms of imagery, signalling the quest for autonomy and the rejection of both neoliberal orthodox recipes and the impositions of international financial institutions.

The arrival of Kirchner, like that of Lula, paved the way for the return of the state's dynamic role in the economy after two decades of neoliberal experimentation and state withdrawal. This was neither statism nor interventionism, but rather a re-evaluation of the vital role of the state as driver of both economic and social development. Kirchner renegotiated some of the over-generous conditions (low royalties, limited investment in infrastructure, no control over prices to consumers) that privatization contracts had granted to private companies, mainly foreign ones. By claiming to be a new arrival, even though he had actually been in politics and in a position of authority for many years, Kirchner was able to draw a line under the errors of the previous administrations and promote himself as champion of the moralization of the state. He whittled down the Supreme Court and spring-cleaned the police and armed forces. He also annulled some of the pardons given by the previous administration to the military involved in gross human rights abuses during the dictatorship and restarted trials for human rights violations. In social affairs, Kirchner prioritized the fight against poverty, inequality and unemployment. This corresponded with events in other Latin American countries and – perhaps ironically – the guidelines of major international bodies, who were now advocating the fight against inequality as a more effective method of fighting poverty than mere economic growth.

Kirchner's mandate was overall a success, but ongoing challenges remained. In the economy, it remains to be seen how far the good results were due to careful management and how far they can be attributed to high prices of export products and the low starting point following the 2001 crisis. In the political domain, Kirchner accorded greater powers to the presidency in order to bypass Argentine society's outmoded resistance to the process of reform. However, this led to a significant concentration of power, lack of debate, and cases of mismanagement and conflict of interest. The risk was that popularity could transform itself into neo-populism with somewhat obscure democratic procedures.

Néstor Kirchner decided not to stand for re-election in 2007 but instead to support the presidential ambitions of his wife, Cristina Fernández Kirchner. Cristina Kirchner is in fact a politician in her own right, not simply by marital association, but her clear victory in the presidential elections raised some questions. What would be the roles of the *presidenta* and the ex-president? Was such a concentration of power in one family desirable? Would Cristina opt for continuity or change following her husband's mandate? The first three years of Cristina's rule maintained major traits of continuity in economic policy and a slight adjustment of foreign policy, where the *presidenta* sought less strained relations with investors and international agencies. However, her mandate has been characterized by numerous challenges and economic and social conflicts following attempts to reform agricultural export taxation (*retenciones*) and growing concerns about corruption scandals and mismanagement of public resources. Former president Néstor Kirchner's influence on government action has been both lasting and considerable. The formula seemed to be *matrimonialism*, a cheerful neologism concocted by the Argentine press which sees wife as head of the executive and husband as head of the party with a relative majority. A significant change of scenario occurred when Néstor Kirchner suddenly died in October 2010 and Cristina Kirchner was left to govern by herself. In spite of growing criticism, the legacy of her husband's policies to tackle poverty and unemployment, the fragmentation and paucity of the opposition, together with sustained economic growth and the pledge to redistribute wealth gave Cristina a comfortable re-election in 2011.

Chile

Chile was the last major South American country to return to democracy and move on from the authoritarian regimes of the 1970s. However, it had one great advantage compared to nearby Brazil and Argentina: a stable and profitable economy, which allowed the newly elected authorities to focus on democratic consolidation with much less concern for economic performance and restructuring. The military regime which came to power in 1973 after a *coup d'état* led by General Augusto Pinochet announced its intention of converting to a 'protected democracy' in 1977, but the process truly began with the drafting of the new constitution in 1980, incorporating detailed articles on the transition. According to this constitution, Pinochet would serve as president for eight more years, after which commanders of the armed forces were to nominate the next presidential candidate whose name would be submitted to a plebiscite. If the plebiscite were successful, the military candidate for the presidency would be confirmed, parliamentary elections would follow and the constitution would be applied in full; if defeated, free elections both for the presidency and parliament would be called. The military agreed to ensure respect for these stipulations, convinced that the 1988 plebiscite would vote Pinochet in for another mandate.

Instead, the plebiscite called for an end to the authoritarian regime. The opposition, which had failed to uproot the military from power despite large-scale demonstrations and popular support, raised its game and created a coalition for a NO vote at the plebiscite. The coalition became known as the *Concertación*. This group brought together opposition parties from across the political spectrum with the exception of the Communist Party, and was largely dominated by the Christian Democrat and Socialist parties. The opposition won the plebiscite with almost 55 per cent of votes and remained united in the resulting presidential elections, presenting a single candidate: Christian Democrat Patricio Aylwin. Aylwin won the 1989 elections and the opposition gained an absolute majority in the lower house but not in the Senate, where senators appointed by the military government still held sway.

As unpleasant as it may sound, the stability and success of the export-based economy under the *Concertación* governments from 1990 until 2010 can be largely attributed to the legacy of the military government. After taking power, Pinochet reversed the unsustainable statist economic order begun under the Allende government, instead entrusting the management of the economy to a group of young neoconservative and liberal economists schooled at the University of Chicago in the United States, known as the Chicago Boys. The group implemented a drastic programme of public deficit reduction and structural reform. The privatization process was broad, but did not apply to strategic sectors such as copper mines, which remained under public control. The economy was opened up to external markets with the lowering of trade barriers and reduction of restrictions on the financial system, and inflation fell significantly.

The process of economic renewal conducted by the military was neither linear nor without its costs. Success was achieved in the long term only after a series of attempts and corrections, and the short-term social costs could be swept aside only because the reforms took place under a dictatorship. At the beginning of the 1980s, in particular, the model needed intensive revision because of rising foreign debt, excess imports and unemployment. This resulted in the so-called 'pragmatic neoliberalism', which blended measures for stimulating the internal market with tariff increases and the reduction of foreign debt. The result was spectacular, and between 1985 and 1997 the Chilean economy grew at an annual rate of over 7 per cent.[13] In this way the *Concertación* governments took the fundamental principles of a successful neoliberal model and gradually and progressively adjusted it to focus greater attention on social affairs. Under the *Concertación* governments, the percentage of poor has dropped by half to about 20 per cent of the population, GDP has almost doubled and inflation now stands at 3 per cent, on a par with that of developed countries.[14] Consolidating democratic institutions, on the other hand, has proved a much more laborious task.

National reconciliation and the punishment of human rights violators by the military were two of the major problems. Aylwin established a Truth and Reconciliation Commission comprising representatives from all political groups, which compiled a report and documented around three thousand cases of missing people. The families of *desaparecidos* received state compensation in the form of lifelong pensions, study grants and free medical treatment. Another commission was established to investigate torture cases and concluded that around thirty-five thousand people had been tortured under the military regime. The *Concertación* government reinterpreted the laws on amnesties that had been enacted by the military before they left power, making them much more restrictive and adopting new laws to allow previously archived cases to be reopened.

The case of Pinochet himself was particularly controversial. Following his defeat in the plebiscite, he retained his post as commander of the armed forces until 1998, in accordance with the constitution. Although requests later began to surface to put the general on trial, he benefited from parliamentary immunity in his position as senator for life, a position allocated to former presidents. In 1998, Pinochet was arrested in London with a warrant issued by a Spanish judge. The debate surrounding his arrest had not only legal but also political implications, and the English, considering the former dictator's ill health, permitted his free return to Chile. Despite widespread support for the waiver of his immunity, Pinochet could not be tried on health grounds and passed away in 2006 without ever paying for the crimes he committed, ordered or even simply tolerated.

Another problem which the *Concertación* governments needed to resolve was the constitutional heritage left behind by the military. The 1980 constitution was authoritarian and granted significant privileges to the military, some of which conflicted with democratic principles. Several amendments were introduced early on with the return to democracy in 1989 but other vital issues remained, such as the overwhelming number of senators who were not elected but nominated by various authorities (including the armed forces via the National Security Council), the role of the National Security Council, which could convene and demand that the president account for his actions in numerous areas, and the president's inability to remove military top brass. As time passed and tensions dwindled between the right, which sympathized with the army, and the centre-left parties of the *Concertación*, the Congress was able to correct all of these constitutional anomalies in 2004, forcing the armed forces to fully submit to civilian authority and completing the political transition to democracy.

Politically speaking, the *Concertación* has been an undoubted success. Democratic stability and continuity have been maintained. In 1994 President Aylwin ceded power to another Christian Democrat, Eduardo Frei (son of the 1960s president Eduardo Frei), who in turn handed over to socialist Ricardo Lagos in 2000. He passed the baton to the first female president of the country, socialist Michelle Bachelet, in 2006. The key to this success is Chilean society's universal consensus on the pursuit of progress and prosperity within a democratic structure, whose interruption in the 1970s can be attributed to the errors and excesses of all players from across the Chilean political spectrum.[15]

From an economic point of view too, the *Concertación* has had notable successes. The post-1990 democratic administrations left untouched the framework of fiscal probity and economic openness handed down by the military and injected democratic credibility into it. Most of all they emphasized the social issues and the fight against poverty. Since the return to democracy, spending on health, education and public building has mounted consistently, wages and minimum pensions have significantly grown, improvements have been carried out on road, maritime and airport infrastructures, trade union conflicts have been appeased and foreign investment has flooded into the country. These measures were boosted by a pragmatic and successful foreign policy which led to free trade agreements with the United States, the European Union, China and South Korea among many others. The country's continuing profound economic inequality was the only sore point. Ideas began to form about the need for a substantial and courageous political change to tackle this problem.

The election of Michelle Bachelet to the presidency in 2006 seemed to be a response to this widespread demand. The pink tide seemed to have arrived in Chile, but in fact there is no better case than Chile to demonstrate how heterogeneous and vague in definition the so-called pink tide really is. Like Lula, Michelle Bachelet also espoused radical and reformist principles early in her career. However, her action in government has been characterized by elements of continuity rather than of change from previous administrations. After being arrested during the dictatorship and exiled first to Australia then to former East Germany, Michelle Bachelet began studying medicine, completing her studies after her return to Chile. A member of the Socialist Youth even before her exile, the future president rejoined the left-wing opposition after coming back to her native country. After the return to democracy, she was employed by the Ministry of Health before going back to university in Chile and then the United States, to complete military and defence studies. She then moved into the Ministry of Defence, before being unexpectedly nominated minister for health by President Lagos in 2000 and later becoming minister for defence in 2002.

In power, Bachelet did maintain her pre-election stances on participatory democracy and female empowerment (including giving equal numbers of cabinet posts to men and women in her government), but generally she followed the example of her predecessors in terms of policy. The economy was entrusted to skilled experts from the neoliberal school. Limits imposed by the coalition nature of the government avoided potentially dangerous radical slips. The few really innovative measures proposed by Bachelet met with considerable resistance and suffered from criticism at least as much as the government's supposed lack of effort to improve the education system. In terms of practical results achieved by Bachelet's administration, the record is also mixed. Although the pension system reform seems to have met with widespread approval, the same cannot be said for the reform of the transportation system in the capital. What's more, Bachelet's ministerial experience and history of militancy did not accord well with her self-promotion as someone new and external to traditional politics.

During twenty years of *Concertación*, Chile has made great progress in achieving a stable, democratic political system and a successful economic model that it is now trying to meld with an efficient, redistributive social policy. However, twenty years of centre-left administrations have prompted in the country a desire for change, faster modernization, and more widespread and tangible benefits of what is still unanimously considered a successful model.

These factors led to the victory of Sebastián Piñera in the 2010 presidential election, which marked the end of twenty years of *Concertación* and the return to power of the right for the first time since the Pinochet years. A tycoon who made his fortune by introducing credit cards in Chile and who has business interests in television and air transportation, Piñera promised to concentrate on job creation and social development. However, the action of his government has so far been characterized by continuity with his predecessors, for three main reasons. First, Chile is becoming a mature democracy where both left and right moderate their positions to appeal to the centre, thus diluting major differences in their political programmes, especially in terms of economic policy. Secondly, the terrible earthquake that hit Chile in 2010, precisely during the transition of power, forced the newly elected government to focus on emergency intervention and reconstruction, thus neglecting some aspects of the original platform. Finally, and perhaps most importantly, the legacy of the *Concertación* is no doubt a very positive one. Its economic and social policies were quite successful although perceived as slightly cautious. The Chilean model needs adjustment towards more equality and redistribution rather than a radical reform.

Venezuela

Of all the pink tide leaders, President Hugo Chávez of Venezuela has perhaps inspired the greatest interest and debate abroad. This is due not only to his radical rhetoric and projects, but also because Venezuela is one of the world's main crude oil producers and because Chávez has somehow embodied the battle between globalization and anti-globalization. It is interesting to note that the most radical turnarounds have taken place in countries like Venezuela and Bolivia, where the application of the neoliberal formula has been least successful. Conversely, there seems to be no unequivocal or direct link between historical conditions of exploitation and long-term crises on the one hand and the emergence of more or less radical progressive regimes on the other. In fact Venezuela was relatively well positioned at the start of the 1980s compared with many Latin American countries, while Bolivia suffered much more from the chronic problems of the continent, such as poverty, inequality, political instability and a tendency to authoritarianism, not to mention the marginalization of indigenous populations.

Unlike many Latin American countries, Venezuela enjoyed a record period of democratic political stability and sustained economic development in the 1970s. At the end of the Pérez Jiménez dictatorship in 1958, the *puntofijismo* system (based on a power-sharing agreement between the two main political parties) was inaugurated. Even with a rigid and elitist political structure, the country was able to prosper thanks to the oil boom and strong state participation in the economy, reaching levels of development, industrial diversification and living standards which were envied by the rest of the continent. However, these improvements were coupled with diffuse corruption, an unwieldy and inefficient patronage system and continual voter manipulation in order to ensure the system's survival. When oil prices fell in the 1980s, Venezuela entered a phase of deep economic stagnation which drastically reduced living standards among the middle class and dragged the less well off into even worse poverty, resulting in a profound political crisis. By the end of the 1980s Venezuela was almost on a par with many of its neighbouring countries in terms of inflation and unemployment, growing poverty and political inertia.

Consequently Venezuela decided to adopt neoliberalism. In 1989, President Pérez began shock treatment to deregulate exchange rates, interest rates and price controls in key sectors such as transport. Popular discontent erupted immediately and protests escalated into a wave of violence known as the *Caracazo*. In 1992 an attempt at a military coup to overthrow Pérez was led by an army officer named Hugo Chávez. The coup did not succeed in capturing Pérez, nor in obtaining support from the majority of the army. Chávez was imprisoned but became extremely popular, especially among the lower classes, as a champion of the poor and the fight against 'party-centric' corruption. President Pérez was deposed the following year after corruption accusations.

Rafael Caldera, elected in 1993 after a campaign advocating state interventionism, soon converted to neoliberalism too. The Venezuelan crisis was aggravated by over-hasty reforms, inadequate planning and low oil prices. Poverty and unemployment spiralled out of control, inequality set in and social conflict was heightened. By the end of the decade trust in the traditional party system had fallen to a historic low point. The 1998 elections were therefore a probing test for the entire political system and resulted in a landslide which brought former coup commander Hugo Chávez to power, this time legitimately and democratically.

After being pardoned by President Caldera in 1994, Chávez began his own political movement, the Fifth Republic Movement (Movimiento V República, MVR), which aimed to found a new republic by scrapping the party-based system, shaking off perceived international impositions and establishing a truly participatory democracy with the aim of achieving socialism. His politico-philosophical vision blended elements of nationalism, references to Latin America's past (specifically to liberator Simón Bolívar), aspects of the military socialist model of former Peruvian president Velasco Alvarado and various socialist and communist influences. The result is 'twenty-first-century socialism', a hybrid defined only roughly by Chávez but which holds great fascination and appeal for the masses and a certain strand of intellectuals. This motto bears a resemblance at times to 1930s and 1940s populism and at times to Cuba's utopian communism, but Chávez has also shown himself to be a shrewd and even pragmatic politician on more than one occasion.

The first measures adopted by Chávez reflected his electoral promises, including an ambitious project of public works and healthcare improvement, the end of privatizations that had been launched under the previous administrations and the first constitutional reform, aiming to make democracy more participatory while simultaneously adding weight to the presidency. The 1999 constitution made it possible to exercise a vote of no-confidence against the president via popular referendum, fleshed out presidential powers, extended the president's mandate from five to six years and brought in the possibility of immediate re-election. The country was officially renamed the Bolivarian Republic of Venezuela. In 2000, Chávez was re-elected according to the rules of the new constitution, and although international observers were unable to confirm the results, they concluded that the vote reflected popular will.

Inspired by his electoral success and equipped with the extraordinary power to legislate via decree for one year, Chávez rapidly proceeded with his plans. An agricultural reform law forced owners of uncultivated land to choose between state plans for cultivation or dispossession. Another law blocked the privatization of the health system begun by the previous government. The organic law on hydrocarbons proved even more radical and controversial, giving the state a majority stake in every joint venture undertaken with private companies in the oil industry and marking a distinct reversal of the neoliberal government's attempts at liberalization. The opposition, made up of industrial associations, trade unions and traditional parties, fought back with a general strike. In 2002 a permanent general strike was declared in reaction to the government's systematic firing of several of the oil company PDVSA's top managers.

In 2002 a *coup d'état* that was indirectly linked to the extended general strike attempted to depose Chávez. It failed, reinforcing the president and his determination to implement still more radical reforms. Demonstrations led to violent clashes between strikers and supporters of the president in Caracas and the rest of the country, threatening the public order. In a televised speech the head of the armed forces announced the resignation of President Chávez, who was being held on a military base, while Pedro Carmona, president of Fedecámaras (Venezuelan Federation of Chambers of Commerce), assumed the presidential role. This attempt backfired, provoking a strong popular reaction in favour of the legitimate president, and troops faithful to Chávez led popular resistance against the coup to restore the president to power. From then on, both Chávez's actions and rhetoric have assumed rather more radical tones in domestic and foreign policy alike.

Chávez has certainly raised Venezuela's international profile. Whether or not this has truly benefited the country remains open to debate. Although traditionally eager to liberate Latin America from the influence of Washington and therefore opposed to the project of the Free Trade Area of the Americas piloted by the United States, Chávez maintained a relatively moderate approach towards the USA until the attempted coup. Claiming that the USA was directly involved in the attempt (indeed, there are still doubts over Washington's role in the event), Chávez lashed out with ferocious anti-American rhetoric implying an almost personal dislike of George W. Bush, whom he called 'the devil'. But tensions with the United States went beyond issues with the administration then in power. A leading role in OPEC and the battle to keep oil prices high, Chávez's interference and posturing on Colombia and in the fight against drug trafficking, not to mention dubious relationships with Iraq, Libya, Iran and Syria, have cooled relations between Venezuela and the United States. Nevertheless, these tensions have not stopped the USA remaining Venezuela's number-one trade partner during

Chávez's thirteen years in government, nor have they prevented the president from signing or renewing various oil agreements between the two countries. The alliance with Cuba, the quest for a decisive role in Latin American regional politics, the proposal for an alternative regional cooperation project to those currently in existence (see Chapter 2) and support for ideologically similar regimes elsewhere on the continent have all coloured relations with nearby states, which are interested in cooperating on energy matters but also have reservations and fears.

On the domestic front, emboldened by his victory in the 2004 recall referendum and the extensive support for his re-election in 2006, Chávez tried to adopt another constitutional reform with a view to establishing twenty-first-century socialism. The bill would notably increase presidential powers, suspend key elements of the rule of law during periods declared as emergencies by the government, limit the autonomy of the Central Bank and place parts of the country's territory, declared of national interest, under direct presidential control. The bill would also allow the unlimited re-election of the president for seven-year mandates. Finally, the inclusion of so-called communal councils in the constitutional framework aimed to devolve, according to the Chávez vision, a slice of power directly to the people. While none of these individual suggestions is intrinsically anti-democratic per se, the bill in its entirety, when accompanied by Chávez's governing style, a significant degree of media control, and the profound polarization in Venezuelan society produced fears and premonitions of an authoritarian swing. The opposition's new-found solidarity coupled with the disenchantment of Chávez supporters (resulting in high levels of abstention among pro-government voters) brought about a victory, albeit a limited one, against Chávez when the adoption of the constitutional text was rejected by a general referendum. This vote defeat was a first for Chávez. However, another referendum in 2009 approved the option of indefinite re-election of the head of state.

Results after thirteen years of the Chávez government are varied. According to *Le Monde Diplomatique*, there have been successes in terms of political inclusion, restoration of dignity and visibility to marginalized peoples and the reinforced role of the state in the economy and society.[16] The results that have most affected daily existence include improvements in the education and healthcare sectors and the drop in poverty. Despite the vicious statistics war between the government and the opposition, even Chávez's opponents acknowledge some considerable achievements. Poverty fell from 40 per cent in 1997 to around 27 per cent in 2007, according to government sources.[17] Social programmes (*misiones*) seem to have produced noteworthy effects. The *Misión Barrio Adentro*, bolstered by Cuban medical staff, has improved healthcare, particularly in the most deprived areas. The *Misión Robinson* has lessened the problem of adult illiteracy to some extent, while the *Misión Guaicaipuro* has targeted the protection and promotion of indigenous communities.

Nevertheless, immense problems and challenges remain. Policy is completely geared to and focused on the figure of the president. Chávez's style of governance inspires little trust in international circles. Inflation is the highest in Latin America, according to *The Economist*.[18] Press freedom is endangered, according to Reporters without Borders. The Konrad Adenauer Foundation has denounced the country's lack of democracy. Transparency International reports high levels of corruption. The United Nations Human Development Index pegged Venezuela at seventy-second place in 2007, down from sixty-first in 2001. Crime rates have climbed and the number of murders per 100,000 inhabitants is alarming.[19] The pro-government strand has often contested these indicators.

The question of whether life in Venezuela was better before or after Chávez remains bitterly debated. The deep-seated polarization is not conducive to objective discussion. Although many of the problems in the Venezuelan state and society pre-date the arrival of Chávez, it is equally true that the Bolivarian government has not managed to alleviate many of the country's appalling problems, inequality being the major sticking point. Yet Venezuela is still a democracy, albeit an illiberal democracy whose government exerts a heavy influence over other state powers. The significant dependency on oil has already shown the potentially negative repercussions on the state budget and resources available for Bolivarian social initiatives both domestically and abroad in periods of declining prices. Although Chávez remains solidly in power, a number of factors seem to have paved the way for a range of possible solutions in the run-up to the presidential elections in 2012. Persistent economic and social issues, the consequences of the global crisis and most recently the announcement that President Chávez is suffering from cancer and is going through a long recovery may a have significant impact on the forthcoming election.

Bolivia

Bolivia is one of the countries which best demonstrates Latin American aspirations and ambiguities under more radical pink tide governments. Currently it is still one of the continent's poorest countries despite its copious resources (notably gas), which have often been exploited by foreign hands. A considerable proportion of the population (exact figures as well as the counting methods are contested) is indigenous and the highest rates of poverty, unemployment and underemployment are found among this community.[20] Neoliberal reforms in the 1990s, often perceived as unwanted foreign interference, failed to resolve the country's main problems and in fact made them worse. A lingering sense of frustration often assumes the form of Don Quixote-esque nationalism, lashing out at both the United States and neighbouring countries while ignoring the internal structural faults which are actually at the root of many of the country's issues with underdevelopment.

Following the restoration of democracy in 1982, Bolivian democratic governments had to deal with growing demands from popular movements, the burden of foreign debt accumulated by the military regimes of the 1970s, and the need to modernize the economy via new international agreements which were conditional on neoliberal reforms. The policies of the first democratic president, Siles Suazo, aptly portray these constraints and ties. Initially, he secured the support of the International Monetary Fund through loans aiming to reduce the debt racked up by previous governments. However, the repayment of this debt was so laborious that Suazo was forced to contract social and investment programmes, leading to protests in various sectors of Bolivian society. This in turn compelled the president to discard the reforms for fear of a loss of consensus that would threaten stability. However, his withdrawal of the reforms irritated international creditors and weakened the national macroeconomic framework, leading to hyperinflation in 1985. The ensuing economic and political crisis brought about the president's resignation. His successors in the 1980s suffered similar fates, with the country wavering between neoliberal reforms and social pressures in a state of constant economic and political turmoil.

President Gonzalo Sánchez de Lozada, a staunch believer in neoliberalism, was elected in 1993. To remedy the situation and pay due attention to much-needed reforms, he immediately announced a broad programme of privatizations, including the sale of 49 per cent of the state oil company, of public enterprises in the air and rail transport sectors, of the electricity industry, and the sale of the greater part of the public mining industry to private investors. The consequent restructuring programme occasioned a sharp rise in unemployment and the weakening of trade unions, ironically one of the governing party's power strongholds. In 1997, former dictator Hugo Banzer was elected president of the republic and continued the policies introduced by Sánchez de Lozada, who was later re-elected in 2002. However, popular opposition to the neoliberal policies and to Bolivia's subjugation to the commands of international bodies had reached record levels, causing outbreaks of conflict and violence.

A first front of resistance concerned the policies which the government had implemented, with the aid of the United States, to combat coca farming. In Bolivia, the cultivation and consumption of coca leaves represent a secular tradition, particularly in mountainous and rural areas dominated by indigenous communities, where chewing coca leaves is considered an everyday antidote to fatigue and to the harsh terrain and climate conditions. There is thus a legal coca farming industry producing goods for traditional and strictly local usage, distinct from cultivation for the purposes of refining and producing narcotic substances. With the exponential increase in demand for cocaine in the 1980s in the United States and then Europe, the illegal coca farming industry expanded rapidly, bringing income to previously destitute agricultural families.

Programmes of forced closure for these farms, although an integral part of the international battle against narcotics, ranked supply rather than demand as a prime target, with grave repercussions for the economy and social cohesion of entire rural communities. In Bolivia the problem is particularly acute. At the beginning of the 1990s coca producers began to band together in federations to protect their interests and distinguish between legal and illegal usage of coca leaves, calling for legal uses to be extended. Conflict with the government was inevitable. The claims of these federations coupled with anti-neoliberal protests propelled future presidential candidate Evo Morales into the limelight.

Firm resistance to government policies resurfaced in the late 1990s with protests against the privatization of the water company in Cochabamba, Bolivia's third-largest city. In 1999 the government privatized the water distribution company, handing it over to a multinational group which increased prices by 200 per cent. This was unaffordable for most of the area's population and protest demonstrations paralysed Cochabamba for several months, forcing the government to renege on the contract with the multinational corporation and reduce charges to their original levels. Over the next few months, the whole country was rocked by popular demonstrations, street barricades and strikes against policies adopted by the government on wages, agriculture and coca eradication.

The situation deteriorated when Sánchez de Lozada returned to power in 2002. New and even more violent protests broke out across the country. The presidency's plan to boost national income by selling gas abroad met with strong resistance. The opposition asked that Bolivian gas be supplied first and foremost to Bolivians without access and that pipelines avoid taking a route through Chile, which was held responsible for Bolivia's loss of access to the sea as the result of the Pacific War in 1884. This assortment of socialist and nationalist demands and uprisings in the rural and indigenous communities led to Sánchez de Lozada's resignation and a profound institutional crisis.

Presidential elections in 2005 unfolded in a climate of uncertainty and tension both nationally and abroad, with pressures in favour of and against candidate Evo Morales. A leader of Aymaran ethnicity, he promised to renationalize the hydrocarbons sector, restore national dignity and autonomy, introduce social policies focusing on the poor and indigenous populations, and write a new constitution underlining these principles. Born in the highlands, Morales had moved to the eastern countryside with his family in order to earn a living by growing crops, including coca. As an eyewitness to the conditions of rural peasants and indigenous communities, he formulated his own ideas and political strategies and by the mid-1990s was the recognized leader of the coca farming federations. After winning a seat in parliament in 1997 he immediately founded the Movement for Socialism (Movimiento al Socialismo, MAS), a party whose propositions included nationalizing industry, legalizing coca farming and equitably redistributing the country's resources. In December 2005 Morales won the election with an absolute majority of 54 per cent of votes.

President Morales wanted to break with tradition and present himself as a new leader from a truly humble background in both word and deed. Before his official inauguration ceremony in the capital city, La Paz, he asked for an additional power conferment ceremony to be held at an archaeological site in accordance with the ancient customs of his ethnic group the Aymara. In stark contrast to the gaudiness and formality of his predecessors, Evo Morales often stands out for his simplicity, even in official ceremonies. At his presidential inauguration he chose a basic white shirt instead of a jacket and tie, and he often turns up at public events and on trips abroad wearing a simple alpaca pullover. The priorities of his administration included rewriting the constitution, nationalizing land and underground resources and redirecting Bolivian foreign policy, which often toed the Washington party line in the 1990s.

The bill for a new constitution has been approved but has created more problems than it has solved. The work of the constituent assembly has prompted sometimes violent clashes between majority and opposition, resulting in the opposition's continual rejection of the bill. Unable to obtain the two-thirds consensus needed for the assembly to pass the bill, the government forced an approval based on simple majority, which the opposition disputed. In truth only a minority of articles were contentious, but these concerned crucial areas, namely the close relationship between the autonomy of provinces and the management and proceeds of natural resources. While the government is seeking to centralize gas profits, the provinces are demanding a larger share of the royalties through reinforced political and economic decentralization.

A striking dualism is emerging in the country: while the poor and mostly indigenous populations in the western highlands are generally favourable to the Morales government, the prosperous eastern regions are anxious for autonomy from the central government and swell the ranks of the opposition. Opinions on the constitutional reform amply reflect this dilemma. Supporters of the text stress that it would reinforce the rights of indigenous populations and concede a certain degree of political and legal autonomy to traditional indigenous communities. Conversely, critics claim that the text weakens property rights, unduly increases the role of the state in the economy and would wrongly and dangerously make equivalence between national tribunals and traditional community courts in legal matters. Moreover, according to the opposition, the text does not explicitly guarantee the regional autonomy highly prized by rich eastern provinces where most of the country's gas fields are located.

The clashes and violent conflicts caused by the wrangling over the constitution have led to three popular referenda which seem to have calmed the storm but have failed to resolve the fundamental issues. In the summer of 2008 the government called for two referenda to confirm confidence in the president and the governors of rebel provinces respectively. Although regarded as the main protagonists of the political conflict, the administrations in office have been confirmed by popular vote both centrally and regionally. Nonetheless, the dispute has still not been settled either way. A third popular referendum in late 2009 finally paved the way for the definitive approval of the constitutional text, without ever resolving the tensions between the central government and the eastern provinces on regional autonomy and the usage of resources.

Controversy has also broken out over the Morales government's measure to renationalize hydrocarbons. Morales stressed that this initiative did not amount to expropriation but rather would bring the control of resources, namely the majority stake in joint ventures or privatized companies, back into state hands. The decree also substantially increases the royalties which foreign companies will have to pay to the government on their profits. As an incentive to accept the terms of this new offer, Morales sent the army to occupy over fifty gas extraction plants and two refineries. All of the foreign companies involved came to an agreement with the government. However, this manoeuvre did little to improve international relations for an executive that had come to power with widespread support and recognition in public opinion both at home and abroad. This energy policy, added to Morales' ambiguity in the fight against drugs trafficking (yes to coca, no to cocaine), has driven Bolivia to redefine its international alliances.

La Paz's position in the continent and within the international community is experiencing a significant change. One of the Morales government's first actions was an international tour to forge new alliances, and indicators show clear attempts to establish links with Europe and China in order to reduce the traditional dependency on the United States. Morales has always taken an anti-neoliberal stance and thus rejected Washington's proposals, especially for the Free Trade Area of the Americas. With an increasingly assertive discourse and a much-publicized alliance with Hugo Chávez, Morales has defined the United States and its allies as an axis of evil, which has done little to maintain cordial relations with some European countries. On a regional level, he has identified Venezuela and Cuba as strong allies because of their ideological similarities and has worked with them on an alternative regionalist programme (see Chapter 2). Bolivia has benefited from Venezuela's generosity in technical assistance and cooperation in the oil sector. Resurgent energy nationalism has, however, sparked tensions with Brazil and Peru, while relations with Chile seem to be going through a phase of more constructive dialogue, especially concerning the creation of a corridor allowing Bolivia to access the Pacific Ocean. Morales' alliance with Chávez, however, has, rightly or wrongly, caused unease in several chancelleries.

The 2009 elections confirmed Morales in the presidency and conferred his party a two-thirds majority in both houses. Although Morales has been very active during his first mandate, results remain mixed and his policy on natural resources provoked national and international perplexity as well as preoccupation about the treatment of some indigenous communities such as the Guarani. It is true that reforms need time to take effect and generate benefits, but the second mandate is expected to deliver on all electoral promises, such as poverty reduction, the redistribution of wealth and land reform. The bar has been set quite high.

An overview of the rest of Latin America

The pink tide, after a temporary slowing down with the 2010 election of conservative candidates Piñera in Chile and Santos in Colombia, seems to have regained vigour with the election of progressive leader Ollanta Humala in Peru in 2011. Regimes hailed as centre-left with deeply reformist aspirations have taken office almost everywhere in South America – with the notable exception of Chile and Colombia, whose reformist credentials are equally solid nonetheless – as well as some Central American countries such as Nicaragua and Guatemala. Also, in Mexico, progressive politician Manuel López Obrador has enlivened politics and electoral campaigns despite failing to win presidential elections. Overall these events demonstrate a newly acquired awareness by Latin American political and economic elites of the need for deep reform to fight social and economic inequality. The consensus on eliminating inequality to pursue a more prosperous, stable and harmonious society seems to transcend the right–left boundaries and debates. In spite of sectors of resistance and the long road ahead, this appears to be the common denominator of a majority of Latin American administrations at the beginning of the twenty-first century.

Uruguay, a small country of great democratic and liberal traditions, suffered repression and dictatorship in the 1970s before returning to democracy in 1984 under the guidance of President Julio María Sanguinetti. In the early 1990s his successor, Luis Alberto Lacalle, also a seemingly traditional party politician, took steps to reform the state and economy along neoliberal lines, simultaneously signing the country up to the new subregional integration agreement Mercosur along with Argentina, Brazil and Paraguay. Protest and popular resistance to the austerity measures resulted in a national agreement between the two traditional parties on the type of economic policies to be implemented. This laid the foundations for Sanguinetti's re-election as president in 1994 and an inclination of the country's policies towards right-of-centre and neoliberal precepts. Despite some improvements to the economic situation, mainly thanks to the financial sector and tourism, President Jorge Battle (1999–2005) was similarly unable to successfully tackle deeply rooted problems such as foreign debt, inflation, unemployment and the worryingly high rates of emigration in a country of just 3.5 million inhabitants. Meanwhile, a progressive coalition – the Frente Amplio – emerged in opposition to the traditional parties. The coalition was led by the former mayor of the capital city Montevideo, Tabaré Vázquez. With a moderate agenda which played down the more radical aspects of neoliberalism and advocated the reinforcement of state intervention in social policies, Vázquez was victorious in 2005 and became the first socialist president in the history of Uruguay. Since then, a combination of good economic management and high export prices has helped Uruguay to drastically reduce its levels of poverty and unemployment. José Mujica, also of the Frente Amplio, succeeded Vázquez in 2010, promising a line of continuity which has enabled Uruguay to maintain economic growth and social improvement.

Paraguay experienced one of the longest dictatorships in history before its difficult return to democracy in the 1990s. The regime of Alfredo Stroessner kept an iron grip on the country from 1954 until 1989, when a coup led by General Rodríguez sparked the democratization process. The 1990s were turbulent for both the economy and politics. The decade recorded the murder of a vice-president and a serious attempt at a *coup d'état* in 1996, which was thwarted by popular resistance and more importantly international pressure. After the election of Nicanor Duarte Frutos as president in 2003, the country enjoyed a degree of economic and political stability, but the dilemmas of unemployment, a depressed economy and social inequality remained. In this context, and after the Partido Colorado's seventy years in power, the arrival of Fernando Lugo as head of state in 2008 opened up new horizons. Known for his radical and progressive positions inspired by liberation theology, Lugo based his electoral campaign on anti-politics and the defeat of corrupt oligarchies, appealing to Paraguayan nationalism to oppose the United States and nearby powerful Brazil. For now he seems to have gained consensus, especially among the poor. In its first term the government has targeted four areas: agrarian reform, fiscal reform, the battle against corruption, and the renegotiation of energy agreements with Brazil. This agenda raised high expectations but also engendered growing social and political tensions, without yet making any significant progress. Lugo's party does not have a majority in either chamber. Whether the government will resist domestic pressures throughout its mandate remains to be seen.

In the Andean region, Ecuador, ravaged by economic backwardness, political instability and deep social inequality, has also begun taking steps towards pink reformism. The transition to democracy in 1979, the oil boom which began in the 1970s and even the (albeit incomplete) implementation of neoliberal reforms in the 1990s have all fallen short of producing the desired results in economic and social development. Ecuadorean politics, especially since the 1990s, have been characterized by the strong involvement of social movements, particularly indigenous ones. The Confederation of Indigenous Nationalities of Ecuador (Confederación de Nacionalidades Indígenas del Ecuador, CONAIE) and subsequently the Pachakutik Plurinational Unity Movement (Movimiento de Unidad Plurinacional Pachakutik) have been bastions of the battle for political and cultural rights for indigenous populations and against neoliberal austerity measures and reforms. Even when forms of these movements came to power, results were disappointing. The pro-indigenous and populist coalition which won the elections in 2002, bringing Lucio Gutiérrez to power, did not manage to reverse the neoliberal reforms brought in by the previous administrations. The dollar continues to be the country's official currency as it attempts to combat spiralling inflation. Dependence on foreign capital and imports remains high, as do social tensions engendered by discontent with these policies. In 2006 Rafael Correa, an outsider not formally linked to any party, won the elections with promises of a social revolution in favour of the less well off. Among his first measures were distancing Ecuador from the United States and aligning more closely with Venezuela and Bolivia. Correa has criticized Washington and rejected the bilateral free trade treaty with the USA, and decided not to renew agreements for a US military base on Ecuadorean soil in Manta. He has also censured policies to eradicate coca farms using pesticide sprays in nearby Colombia, claiming that this would harm legal coca farms on the border with his country. In Ecuador, there is thus a palpable tension between rhetoric and pragmatism. Despite Correa's criticism of the Free Trade Area of the Americas and the bilateral free trade agreement with the United States, he supported the US Andean Trade Promotion and Drug Eradication Act (ATPDEA), which gives Ecuador vital access to preferential tariffs on the US market. In 2008 the new constitution bolstering presidential powers was approved with a large majority and Correa comfortably won re-election in 2009. After being held by protesting policemen in 2010 and being liberated by the armed forces, he has recently achieved through referendum increased presidential powers over the media and judicial appointments. Ecuador is now part of the *chavista* Bolivarian camp and the government has promised to increase public spending in the area of social projects.

In Peru, the 1980s were an extremely turbulent period marked by a pronounced debt crisis and attacks by the terrorist organization Shining Path (Sendero Luminoso). In the second half of the 1980s President Alan García set the scene for an autonomous foreign policy and expansionistic economic policies which, in spite of some initial successes, had collapsed into disaster by the end of the decade. Alberto Fujimori, a university professor from a family of Japanese immigrants who promoted himself as the people's candidate, won the elections in 1990. He activated the drastic and profound neoliberal adjustments which were in vogue at the time, fully embracing economic openness, cutting public spending and privatizing many production sectors. In 1992 he led a coup against his own government, suspending the constitution and adopting widespread powers. Initially the excellent economic results, coupled with the defeat of the Shining Path, generated a degree of domestic consensus and international tolerance. As the economy slowed down and a corrupt and violent regime took hold, Fujimori lost credit and power and was forced to resign in 2001. The new president, Alejandro Toledo, promised a strong commitment to job creation and obtained some good results in economic growth, without, however, making an impact on the profound inequalities in Peruvian society and the poor conditions of much of the Andean and indigenous population.

Peruvian society displayed a strong desire for change in the 2006 elections. Ollanta Humala of the radical left, whose supporters included Hugo Chávez, ran against former president García, who won over his fellow citizens with a more moderate agenda. During his mandate, García adopted austerity measures and took inspiration from the Chilean model, achieving impressive economic growth, job creation and the reduction of poverty, mainly thanks to the export boom and the knock-on effect of Chinese economic growth. The good results obtained by García prompted a widespread desire for the redistribution of the gains. Leftist candidate Ollanta Humala won the 2011 presidential election because he was able to capture this aspiration of Peruvian society while tempering his rhetoric and declaring himself to be a follower of Lula's moderate model of social development with economic stability. After defeating in the run-off the daughter of former president Fujimori, the champion of the right, Humala has now a difficult task ahead: to preserve fast economic growth, tackle inequality effectively and fight against the expansion of coca cultivation and trafficking in Peru.

In Mexico, the Institutional Revolutionary Party (Partido Revolucionario Institucional, PRI) governed the country without interruption from the revolution in the first half of the twentieth century until 2000. Initially buffered by the oil economy and intense trade with the United States, Mexico nonetheless suffered a pronounced economic crisis in the early 1980s, ending in the suspension of debt repayment in 1982 and the introduction of neoliberal reforms between the 1980s and the start of the 1990s. Although it stabilized and relaunched the economy, the neoliberal era had no meaningful impact on inequality, marginalization, the lack of public services, or unemployment. Discontent in the poorest and mostly indigenous areas in the south incited the Zapatista uprising in 1995. Thus true political change was not channelled through socialist regimes or members of the pink tide, but the end of PRI dominance in 2000. For the first time a different party, the National Action Party (Partido de Acción Nacional, PAN), won the elections with Vicente Fox as leader. The transformation that took place was one of principle rather than practice as the PRI, in spite of its rhetoric, had already embraced the economic openness and modernization now endorsed by the PAN. Obstructed by a slender majority in his plans for reform, the Fox administration nonetheless contributed to increased political freedom and improved economic stability and growth, and it vitally boosted a broad social programme called *Oportunidades*. This initiative, inherited from previous PRI governments, was fleshed out and given a finance injection to achieve encouraging results in the fight against poverty and inequality. This demonstrates that such ambitions are not solely the territory of pink tide governments, but are also priorities for the good governance of the continent, regardless of the political ideology of the administration in power. The 2006 elections saw PAN candidate Felipe Calderón face rival Manuel López Obrador, former mayor of Mexico City, representing the Party of the Democratic Revolution. This signalled the arrival of the pink tide in Mexico, which rejected the economic policy of the past twenty years, criticized the Fox government as the rich and powerful elite and instead promised a government for the poor. López Obrador provoked fears among the business sector and the middle classes and the electorate ended up voting in Calderón. He has mainly extended the Fox government's policies and concentrated on social measures, battling drug cartels, crime and tax evasion, and the expansion of infrastructure. However, so far his presidency has been marked by the high cost in human lives and crime rates generated by his firm fight (including the use of the army) against the drug cartels and by the economic crisis following the 2008 financial turmoil and diminished international demand for Mexico's exports, especially from the USA. PAN was penalized by voters in the 2009 mid-term elections, giving hope to the PRI for a possible return to power in 2012.

The only South American country whose political system has not been shaken or challenged by the pink tide is Colombia. Here, social issues are linked more to troubles caused by guerrilla warfare and drug trafficking than the type of government and its economic policy priorities. Perhaps surprisingly, democratic stability and continuity have been among the country's most remarkable features. Colombia also embraced neoliberal reforms in the 1990s, endorsing trade liberalization and privatization, and eliminating subsidies and cutting public spending. Despite some positive results, the country's neoliberal experience faced the same limits found elsewhere. However, Colombia's major dilemma was and remains the complex interlacing of drug trafficking, guerrillas and paramilitary groups, an extremely complicated riddle to solve, which has been dragging on for years and has involved a number of external actors such as the United States and several bordering countries. The internal conflict began in the 1960s. The dominant guerrilla group in terms of size and impact is the Revolutionary Armed Forces of Colombia (Fuerzas Armadas Revolucionarias de Colombia, FARC), a communist-inspired formation with roots in peasant self-defence groups in the 1940s and 1950s. To defend their land from guerrilla attacks, a growing number of landowners resorted to private paramilitary militia. The drug trafficking industry, which initially facilitated, sustained and benefited from both guerrillas and paramilitary militia, is now either carried out by those same organizations, or demands money and other resources in exchange for protection for coca farmers in zones controlled by the guerrillas. President Pastrana, elected in 1998, sought a solution combining military repression with policies for rural development and working towards peace talks, but was forced to back down on peace negotiations in 2002 in light of persistent guerrilla violence. His successor, Álvaro Uribe, opted instead for decisive military action and a relentless battle against the guerrillas. With economic, military and technological support from the United States, the guerrillas were driven into remote areas of the Amazonian jungle and the state regained control of most of the country. In one fell swoop, Uribe also dealt with the problem of drug trafficking by deploying an extensive eradication programme involving spraying illegal coca farms with pesticides. The administration's hard line is paying off. FARC and drug trafficking have not been completely subdued but Colombia, thanks to increased security, has been able to attract foreign investment and achieve steady growth levels during the past few years. After holding several ministerial posts, including the defence brief, in 2010 Juan Manuel Santos succeeded Uribe as president of Colombia. He pledged to continue his predecessor's successful policies against drug trafficking and guerrillas, to develop infrastructure and create more jobs. Among his first successes is the improvement of relations with neighbouring Venezuela.

The pink tide has reached Central America too. In this region, however, improvements have been less evident and consistent than in South America. Poverty and inequality, together with alarming crime and migration problems, still characterize the region at large. In Guatemala, centre-left candidate Álvaro Colom won the 2007 elections. Although he is not ethnically Mayan, he promised to pursue national unity and improve the conditions of the indigenous population (about 40 per cent of the total). Results have been mixed so far and the country remains one of the poorest in Latin America with widespread corruption, high crime rates and low life expectancy.

Honduras has traditionally been plagued by high inequality, serious crime problems and underdevelopment. Hurricane Mitch devastated the country in 1998, thus aggravating many of the country's problems. In 2006 leftist president Manuel Zelaya took office. His presidency was characterized by controversy over his close relations with Hugo Chávez, clashes with the media and attempts to reform the constitution. In 2009 Zelaya was ousted from power with the support of the military. In spite of widespread international protest the interim authorities held an election and new president Lobo Sosa was sworn in. Social and economic problems in Honduras are now coupled with political instability and contested legitimacy.

In El Salvador, after a brutal civil war in the 1980s, peace was restored in 1992. From then until 2009 the conservative ARENA party won every election but was unable to solve or reduce significantly the huge problems of poverty, inequality and crime, and the economy is highly dependent on remittances from Salvadoreans living in the USA. In 2009, Mauricio Funes, a former TV journalist, won the presidency for the leftist party the Farabundo Marti National Liberation Front. Presenting himself as a moderate and a reformist, Funes has re-established diplomatic relations with Cuba, pursued fruitful relations with the USA and pledged to tackle street gangs.

Traditionally one of the poorest countries in the western hemisphere, Nicaragua experienced a leftist revolution led by the Sandinistas in 1979. Stricken by a civil war dictated by Cold War logics in the 1980s, the country returned to peace and democracy in the 1990s. In spite of some economic improvement the situation remained dramatic for most of the population. In 2006 the

Sandinista revolutionary leader Daniel Ortega made a comeback, winning the presidential election. His new stance is much more moderate than in the past. He has pursued close links with Hugo Chávez and other leftist leaders in Latin America but has also come to realize the importance of good relations with the USA and has supported the ratification of the free trade area between the USA and Central America.

After years of dictatorship under General Noriega, Panama returned to democracy in the 1990s. Its economy is largely linked to the Panama Canal, which connects the Pacific and Atlantic oceans, but offshore finance, manufacturing, tourism and banana crops also contribute to a relatively healthy economy whose benefits nonetheless remain very unevenly distributed. To tackle inequality Martín Torrijos of the centre-left was elected president in 2004. His administration focused on social security, fiscal reforms and the project to expand and modernize the Panama Canal. Partly because of the global financial crisis and a slowdown in the economy, and partly because of a perceived rise in prices and crime rates, businessman Ricardo Martinelli won the 2009 elections for the conservative Alliance for Change. His programme includes the attraction of foreign investment, the promotion of free trade and commitment to the expansion of the Canal.

Finally, Costa Rica represents an exceptional case in Central America. The country enjoys a stable political system, a healthy economy, high social standards and has no army. Under social conservative president and Nobel peace laureate Óscar Arias, Costa Rica successfully pursued a moderate free market economic policy between 2006 and 2010. His successor, Laura Chinchilla, the first woman to become president in the country's history, and also from the centrist National Liberation Party, promised a line of substantial continuity. Among the measures announced are an increase in funds for education, the expansion of free trade agreements and a tough stance against drug trafficking, an increasing problem for the country.

Conclusions

The pink tide that has washed over the current political and therefore also economic and social landscape in Latin America is a phenomenon of great complexity and diversity. A common feature is the emphasis on social issues, an aspect neglected by neoliberalism and one of the main reasons it has been challenged as an ideology. However, governments from every political standpoint (from Chile to Brazil, from Mexico to Colombia) are now focusing renewed attention on social matters, particularly the fight against inequality and poverty, with instruments that are more sophisticated, efficient and redistributive than mere economic growth.

Another common feature is the re-emergence of the role of the state in the economy, especially as a driver of social progress. From neoliberal Chile to liberal orthodox Mexico to radical Venezuela, the state (and not the market or economic growth) has been at the heart of strategies for improving society. In some cases this has been accompanied by resurgent nationalism, if not in fact then at least in rhetoric. The resurgence of national interest and discourse has emphasized the restoration of autonomy, dignity and control of one's own resources and future. Often this narrative has served to cement government support. At the same time, similarities in discourse, accompanied by state distribution of services and benefits and a quite personalized approach to politics with evergreen charismatic leaders, are somehow reminiscent of 1930s and 1940s Latin American populism, although in a different domestic and international environment.

Finally, numerous challenges remain. Some of the pink tide regimes are pushing the boundaries of democratic rules in order to advance their own reformist ambitions. How far will they be able to travel down the path of illiberal democracy? Many of the (sometimes spectacular) results obtained by Latin American governments in recent years seem highly dependent on the high prices of raw material exports, which have generated abundant resources for investing in social programmes. If prices were to fall on the international market (and history tells us that commodities and foodstuff prices are subject to cycles, sometimes unpredicted and unpredictable ones), would many of these governments and their reform programmes be able to survive? The 'global' crisis has affected to different degrees both industrialized countries and some emerging economies such as China and Russia. But China and other Asian countries have only briefly slowed down their growth, while Europe and North America have experienced recession and have not fully recovered. Latin America seems to have fared well through the crisis, with Brazil and Peru experiencing spectacular growth and most others performing well. So far China's rise has compensated for the West's decline. But the 'reprimarization'[21] of many Latin American economies may bring unexpected downturns on to the path towards development and generate instead patterns of dependency.

The quality of education and health services remains a major problem in most Latin American countries and a crucial issue for development. Is the current dual system, in place in many Latin American countries, of good-quality private services available to few and low-quality public services affordable to a majority, viable? Will good governance win over corruption and vested interests to ensure a more equitable development? What will be the long-term effects of the current economic and social development model and of an increasingly wide social participation? What will be the repercussions on electoral politics? Consequently, and crucially, should the pink tide be considered a permanent or a temporary phenomenon? There is no easy answer. The neoliberal era, like other eras in history, reveals that political and economic events, phases and turns are cyclical. What seems destined to endure, though, is the national and international focus on the fight against poverty, marginalization and social inequality.

TWO
Latin American regionalism: between unity and diversity

Introduction

The abundance of international cooperation agreements between Latin American countries on a whole host of issues is one of the most remarkable aspects of the political and economic landscape of the American continent. Latin America is second only to Europe in terms of the intensity and extension of the phenomenon of regionalism both in the past and today. The rise of progressive regimes during recent years has had an impact on regional integration too.

At first sight, the term 'regionalism' seems to have a straightforward and obvious meaning, but it is difficult to give a more precise definition. What exactly does regionalism mean? In which terms and by which criteria are regions defined and delineated? The term 'regionalism' is deliberately used in a broad sense in order to describe and make sense of a series of interlinked, but distinct, phenomena. These phenomena take place within a certain geographical area defined as a region and tend to reinforce the perception of that region as a unified area. As Andrew Hurrell of Oxford University noted, while diverse human activities and interactions such as a significant level of interdependency and integration at the societal level, regional awareness or identity and interstate cooperation on a variety of issues all form part of the broad term regionalism, perhaps the best known and most widespread studied aspect of regionalism is *regional economic integration*. This requires a specific political commitment to reduce or remove barriers to the free circulation of goods, services, capital and people within the region.[1] While simple agreements to reduce barriers to exchanges could in themselves constitute an example of regional integration, this tends to assume more complex and sophisticated forms. A free trade area is a space where all tariff and non-tariff barriers to the free movement of goods have been removed. A customs union is a free trade area with an additional common external customs barrier adopted by the members of the union on trade exchanges with third countries. Finally, a common market is a customs union in which significant coordination of the macroeconomic policies of the member countries takes place.

The level at which regionalism operates, or its geographical scope, also needs to be defined. In the case of Latin America, there are three levels, each with specific characteristics that define its limits and horizons. Latin American countries are particularly active in subregional integration schemes which cover more limited geographical areas. For example, the Common Market of the South, Mercosur, including Argentina, Brazil, Uruguay and Paraguay, is a subregional integration scheme in that it covers only part of the geographical macro-region of South America, or the area known culturally as Latin America. The second level is regionalism as it is more commonly perceived, where the geographical area of the member states in the agreement encompasses the entire geographical macro-region (South America, for example) or the cultural macro-region (Latin America). Examples of this include the Latin American Free Trade Association (Asociación Latinoamericana de Libre Comercio), founded in 1960, or the South American Union (Unión Sudamericana, Unasur), founded in 2008. Finally there is the continental level, where Latin American countries square up to and debate with the rich countries of North America: Canada and the United States. The differences in political and economic power between the United States and Latin American countries have made relations between the two, including continental agreements, more difficult and unbalanced. Nevertheless, there is a reasonably functioning 'inter-American' system of international bodies which are active in politics, economic cooperation and human rights.

The roots and development of Latin American regionalism

Institutionalized regionalism has been most successful in Europe and the Americas. Regionalism is most deeply and unshakably rooted in these regions. The formation of a certain sensitivity to, if not exactly awareness of, regionalism and the desire of countries to make the most of their regional location existed long before the formal establishment of any regional organizations. However, only very few of these were formally proposed, discussed and established before the Second World War. Latin American regionalism is an exception to this rule. Latin American attempts at subregional, regional and even continental unity and integration date back to the nineteenth century. The history of Latin American regionalism, at both the subregional and continental levels, is intertwined with that of the relations between the USA and Latin America. The former was so rich in power and influence that it couldn't be ignored. The latter remained highly dependent on the USA and in constant search of an equilibrium.

When Spanish colonies in the New World gained independence in the early 1800s, the newborn South American republics were united by a shared sense of community, history and values. Simón Bolívar, the hero who led the struggle to liberate Latin America from colonial domination, aimed to found a confederation of the new republics. This plan did not have particularly anti-US connotations, as this was in 1815, before the announcement of the 1823 Monroe Doctrine which unilaterally declared the USA's predominance over the American continent. The venture was not to include Brazil, which was still under the Portuguese crown. Unity was considered the only way to economic and social development. In his famous letter from Jamaica, Bolívar stressed the common features of Latin American republics: roots, language, customs and religion. He called for the founding of three Hispanic-American federations: one for Mexico and Central America, one for the northern part of South America and one for the southern part. These three federations would in turn make up a unified Hispanic-American Federation. The idea was discussed by the Congress of Panama in 1826 but failed to gain ground owing to the rise of fierce nationalism in the participating republics and the dwindling threat of Spain's return, which had caused countries to bond during the fight for independence and for some years after.

Another conceptualization of Latin American regionalism was proposed halfway through the nineteenth century by Juan Bautista

Alberdi, an eminent Argentine intellectual and politician. He envisaged the establishment of a Latin American Union. Unity was again perceived as an effective tool towards development. Alberdi's proposal directly opposed the Monroe Doctrine and North American imperialism, and included the participation of Brazil in the project. The aim of this initiative was to keep peace on the continent, remove trade barriers and also introduce a common currency. However, the project was once again compromised by internal rivalries and divisions in the Latin American world. In spite of everything, these preliminary attempts provided fodder for future development. The basic principles, ambitions and even contradictions of contemporary Latin American regionalism were determined in the mid-nineteenth century: the attitude towards the United States, the sometimes ambiguous role of Brazil, and unity and cooperation as drivers for economic and political development.

Several attempts have also been made to unite the whole of the American continent, both North and South. This is known as 'pan-Americanism'. Here, too, the United States has played a key role both in promoting initiatives and in prompting action from Latin Americans, some of whom perceive this as a further attempt at domination by Washington, while others see pan-Americanism as a way to limit US influence over the rest of the continent. This has been and remains an ongoing dilemma within the institutions of the 'inter-American system'.

In 1881, the US Secretary of State, James Blaine, called for an international conference to discuss how to prevent the use of force on the American continent. The aim certainly was to keep the peace, but more importantly to guarantee a favourable environment for the expansion of US industries. Seven years later, Blaine's proposal came to fruition and the first pan-American conference was held. The maintenance of peace, trade development and the economic integration of the continent were all on the agenda. There were no plans for any kind of political cooperation or military alliance. The most daring proposal brought to the table was the creation of a continental customs union, but Latin American delegates rejected this, fearing a loss of national sovereignty. Even Senator Hale's suggestion during discussions at the Washington Senate of a free trade area with Canada and Latin America strictly limited to raw materials had little effect. The USA's aggressive trade policy and economic expansionism in succeeding years, along with its use of military might to boost its power of persuasion, led to the abandonment of pan-Americanism until the end of the Second World War.

Before 1945, experiments with subregional regionalism had also been conducted, such as the attempts in the Southern Cone to establish some kind of institutionalized cooperation between Argentina, Brazil and Chile. The first of these projects dates back to 1905, when the then Brazilian foreign affairs minister Río Branco proposed the ABC Pact (Argentina, Brazil, Chile). Its main aim was to keep the peace between the three countries and define common rules should significant diplomatic friction arise. The plan never got off the ground, essentially because Argentina feared that such an undertaking could damage relations between Buenos Aires and Washington. In 1915, after the US invasion of the Mexican city of Veracruz had strengthened Latin American solidarity, a much less ambitious treaty between the three parties was drawn up but was never ratified because of US pressures on the signatory governments: Washington feared the creation of a bloc hostile to its interests in Latin America.

In 1940 a second attempt took place when the Argentine minister for the economy, Federico Pinedo, proposed a bilateral agreement with Brazil on exports of surplus products from the respective countries. The scope of the agreement was expanded during negotiations and concluded in 1941. It provided for the creation of a customs union which was expressly open to other Latin American countries which might want to be involved in the scheme. The escalation of hostilities in the Pacific and Brazil's entry into the war in 1942, while Argentina remained neutral almost until the end of the conflict, brought about the agreement's downfall. Only after 1945 did new forms of regionalism blossom again in Latin America in the context of a very different regional and international scenario.

Latin American regionalism during the Cold War

The Cold War had significant consequences for Latin America. The attempts of the USA and the Soviet Union to draw as many states as possible into their respective spheres of influence bumped security issues up to the top of the international agenda. From the end of the war to the mid-1950s, regionalism witnessed a resurgence in the Americas, this time coloured or perhaps distorted by the background of the Cold War. The regionalism of that time focused on the continental level, with attempts to construct a solid Western political and military bloc which could not be penetrated by the Soviets. The founding of the Organization of American States (OAS) and the conclusion of the Rio Treaty in 1948 were two such attempts. The former set out guidelines for political coordination between the states of the American continent and essentially became a tool for the USA to promote its interests during the Cold War. The latter was a military defence pact aiming to protect the continent against attacks from third countries, namely the Soviet Union and its allies. While the USA understood these bodies as instruments to bypass the UN and have a free hand in hemispheric affairs, the Latin Americans considered them a guarantee of limited US interference. Divergence in interpretation gave rise to resentment and frictions throughout the Cold War.

A significant change on the international and regional chessboards took place between the late 1950s and the start of the 1960s. The softening of opposition between the blocs following the 'de-Stalinization' of the USSR and renewed international awareness of economic and development issues led to a review of regional cooperation strategies on the American continent. The USA realized that Latin America's loyalty to the Western cause could be bolstered through economic and social development and by fighting poverty.

In the 1950s, the dependency theory was a popular way of explaining and suggesting solutions for the problems of underdevelopment. This theory emphasized the dependency of poor and marginal countries on rich and important ones, and insisted that developing countries should replace imports from rich countries with local production to stimulate development via import substitution. Local industrialization financed by public capital and the protection of the infant domestic industry from foreign competition were central to this approach. This theory had many supporters, including the Argentine economist Raúl Prebisch and the United

Nations Economic Commission for Latin America and the Caribbean (ECLAC).[2] ECLAC promoted the formation of a broad Latin American regional economic aggregation with the scope to expand the market for nascent Latin American industries and screen them from competition from countries with more advanced industries. This regional aggregation would set high external customs barriers for foreign goods to stimulate the expansion of the internal market.

The type of regionalism that emerged from this theoretical framework privileged regional and subregional groupings between Latin American countries favouring South–South cooperation. Between the early 1960s and the 1970s the first wave of institutionalized Latin American regionalism took place with the launch of numerous regional integration schemes. This kind of regionalism was labelled 'closed', given that it aimed to limit exchanges between the regional bloc and the rest of the world in order to promote intra-bloc industry and trade.

In 1960, eleven Latin American countries, including Mexico and the largest countries in South America, signed the Treaty of Montevideo, which founded the Latin American Free Trade Association (LAFTA). The aim was to create a free trade area between the signatory parties, but results were modest, and in 1980 LAFTA was replaced by the Latin American Integration Association (LAIA or Asociación Latinoamericana de Integración, ALADI), whose objectives were decidedly less ambitious.

In 1961 Guatemala, Honduras, Nicaragua and El Salvador signed the Treaty of Managua (the capital of Nicaragua), founding a Central American Common Market (CACM). Costa Rica joined in 1963. The results were noticeably better than those of any other regional scheme during that period, but the depth of economic integration and political coordination was still low. The common market dissolved in 1969 following the outbreak of war between Honduras and El Salvador.

Also in 1969, the countries of the Andean area devised their own regional integration scheme. With the Treaty of Cartagena, Bolivia, Ecuador, Peru, Colombia and Chile set up the Andean Community with the aim of integrating their respective economies and creating a common market. Venezuela signed up to the agreement in 1973 while Chile withdrew in 1976 for reasons connected to Pinochet's dictatorial regime. The results were extremely modest and the scheme lay practically dormant until an attempt was made to revive it in the 1990s. Finally, even the tiny islands of the Caribbean archipelago followed the trend of closed regionalism which was popular in the 1960s and 1970s by founding the Caribbean Community in 1973.

None of these closed regionalism formats generated the desired results, largely because of a series of problems and contradictions common to many of them. Although on the one hand the economy and trade in the countries had improved (albeit not as much as expected), on the other hand the political classes lacked willingness to fulfil their regional commitments. Many countries adopted an ambiguous attitude towards these commitments, preferring instead to retain a degree of freedom in political and economic choices, especially during the recurrent crises. Furthermore, the capital available locally was quite limited and dependency on rich countries for supplies of manufactured goods and technology proved an extremely tough hurdle to surmount. Industrialization then took place through heavy use of foreign capital, which did little to resolve the age-old dependency issue. This situation was exacerbated by the insufficient resources available to Latin American countries to pursue effective integration. In particular, the disposable funds were not commensurate with the ambition and breadth of the aims and objectives of this wave of regionalism. Finally, Latin American economies were pretty similar in terms of productive structure and output, which made them competitors rather than complementary. Structural limitations hindered opportunities for further regional integration.

The 1980s were known as 'the lost decade'. Latin American countries slid into a period of deep economic recession and debt rises which limited efforts towards and resources for development. The regional integration schemes which had been drafted in the 1960s suffered first from the global economic crisis of the 1970s, then from the debt disaster of the 1980s. During this decade only Argentina and Brazil, taking advantage of the concurrent redemocratization process and the waning of the East–West conflict, successfully made progress towards integration and laid the foundations for the creation of Mercosur in the 1990s. Also in the 1990s, a series of historic changes took place in both politics and economics, giving rise to a second wave of Latin American regionalism based on new principles but still aiming to tackle the ever-present problems of economic development and Latin American unity.

From open regionalism to the search for new solutions

The fall of the Berlin Wall and the Soviet empire radically transformed the post-1989 international landscape. At the beginning of the 1990s, the United States was the only remaining global superpower. Consequently the US model, embraced by the Western world, was singularly triumphant and, furthermore, seemed to be the only one available after the downfall of communism. Across the world, bar only a few countries such as Cuba, attempts were made in various ways to conform to this model. Political democracy and free market economy became the fundaments of development, influencing the strategies of states and international organizations. In particular, the major financial institutions based in Washington worked on a development plan called the Washington Consensus, based on the adoption of neoliberal economic policies meant to open up the economy. These measures included large-scale privatizations, removal of trade barriers, reduction of the role of the state, deregulation, and cuts in public spending. Latin America also took this on board. All of its authoritarian regimes except for Cuba gave way to forms of more or less liberal and functioning democracies. All of the countries of Latin America attempted to implement neoliberal economic reforms, prioritizing trade liberalization, privatization and fiscal discipline, albeit eschewing the emphasis that the Washington Consensus had originally placed on the need to channel public spending towards social policies.[3]

Alongside these events, a phenomenon which had already begun some time before started to gather speed: globalization. This term is used to describe the process of greater interconnectedness and interdependence among different regions of the world in the political, economic, cultural, social and environmental domains.[4] Globalization implies a need for national economies to compete on the global level, which means constantly seeking new markets and more efficient strategies to deal with external concerns. For poor and relatively industrialized countries like those of Latin America, the need to pool the resources of the region in order to afford a better response to competition at a global level became a catalyst for the second wave of regionalism in the 1990s.

Furthermore, the end of the Soviet threat meant that the United States could relax its political and economic hold on Latin America, allowing the subcontinent to renew regional cooperation according to its own requirements. In addition, by switching its political and economic focus to eastern Europe and the Middle East after the First Gulf War, the United States provoked fears in Latin America of being excluded from major global trade routes and losing investment. The regional aggregation presented a possible method for mitigating these dangers. As it had to deal with an increasingly interconnected world and the challenges of globalization, 1990s Latin American regionalism was defined as open regionalism, in that it did not aim to isolate the region from the rest of the world; on the contrary, it aimed to make it more open and competitive at a global level, capable of squaring up to and overcoming challenges and problems of global proportions.

Thus in the 1990s both subregional and continental regionalism flourished once again. The United States seemed to have adopted a more open and cooperative attitude towards Latin America compared to its previous stance. New integration schemes were introduced and existing ones were rejuvenated. In particular, Mercosur emerged as the most relevant political and economic scheme for Latin America, while NAFTA brought to light new challenges and problems, being the first economic integration agreement between North and South and encompassing vastly diverging cultures and traditions such as those of the United States and Mexico. Other schemes were adjusted and implemented, and the inter-American system was given a new lease of life and an injection of vitality.

This enthusiasm lasted for about a decade. At the beginning of the new millennium it became apparent that many of the long-standing problems of development and social inclusion were still yet to be resolved, the recurrent economic crises had not yet been confined to the past, and the actions of the United States still, quite understandably, promoted its own interests first and foremost. The limits of neoliberalism, the economic crises in Brazil and Argentina, the waning of pan-American enthusiasm and the need to focus greater attention on social needs, along with the accession to power of progressive administrations, all contributed to the need to reformulate Latin American regionalism for the twenty-first century.

Mercosur

The Common Market of the South (Mercosur) is by far the most sophisticated, long-lasting and successful example of regional integration involving Latin American countries, despite its ever-present limits and contradictions. Mercosur is a regional integration bloc which includes Argentina, Brazil, Paraguay and Uruguay. Venezuela officially joined in 2006, but at the time of going to press the ratification procedure has yet to be concluded. Mercosur is the direct outcome of a closer diplomatic relationship and bilateral economic integration between Argentina and Brazil, the two giants of the Southern Cone. Its formation thus generated two major consequences for its own future: first, the Mercosur model is largely following in the footsteps of the outlines and basic principles of the Argentina–Brazil integration model, especially with its essentially intergovernmental nature and the lack of any truly supranational institutions or powers. Secondly, the two countries play a decisive role in the agreement. This is true both for the management of current affairs and the planning of future development and evolution.[5]

During the second half of the 1970s, international relations in the Southern Cone seemed somewhat strained and were not conducive to attempts at cooperation. Argentina and Brazil were involved in a series of diplomatic scuffles over the use of the Paraná river's water resources. Argentina and Chile were on the brink of war over the delimitation of territorial boundaries on the continent's southernmost coast. Uruguay and Paraguay were dipping in and out of the Argentinian and Brazilian spheres of influence, hoping to get as much as possible from their links to both. The situation was exacerbated by the presence of military regimes which, with their essentially geopolitical and security-based view of international relations, erred on the side of conflict rather than solidarity with their neighbours. Finally, the economic crisis and the decline of the import-substitution-based development model made for a rather fragile regional equilibrium.

Ironically, it was the desire to overcome these negative circumstances which gave Argentina and Brazil the motivation to take steps to strengthen diplomatic ties. On the Argentinian side, the worsening crisis with Chile and the deteriorating domestic political situation forced the military junta to reinforce relations with Brasilia. In Brazil, economic stagnation and the need to find new energy supplies encouraged the government to seek an agreement with the Argentines. In 1979 Argentina and Brazil signed the Itaipu Treaty, heralding a phase of cordial and friendly relations between the two countries which has lasted until the present time.

The first half of the 1980s was characterized by the deepening of the economic crisis on the continent and the return of Argentina, Brazil and Uruguay to democracy. Economic modernization and democratic consolidation seem to have been the triggers for the bilateral economic integration process initiated by Argentina and Brazil. In November 1985 the two countries announced their intention to undertake a bilateral integration process, and in July 1986, after six months of intense and mostly secret negotiations, the Buenos Aires Act formally established a system of sectorial protocols – a total of twenty-four were signed – to gradually and flexibly reduce customs barriers on bilateral trade. In 1988, the Argentina–Brazil Treaty of Integration announced the constitution of a free trade area within ten years. However, at this juncture the initial motivation seems to have petered out and the system of protocols soon ran out of production sectors with a significant interest in integration.

The big political and economic changes of the late 1980s and early 1990s brought about the definitive drive towards the constitution of Mercosur. The new neoliberal presidents, Collor in Brazil and Menem in Argentina, were at the heart of the Mercosur project. As advocates of broad, swift liberalization and economic openness, the two presidents decided to transform the bilateral integration project into a global competition tool for the whole of the Southern Cone. In their view, a competitive and open regional single market would be able to attract investments previously directed at transition economies and would give the region political gravitas on the world stage.[6] The constitution of the bilateral common market in 1990 was a precursor to the aggregation of Uruguay and Paraguay (the latter had returned to democracy in 1989). The Treaty of Asunción in 1991 founded Mercosur and planned to make the common market operational by 1995.

The desires for democratic consolidation and subregional unity have always been two fundamental aspects of Mercosur. However, over time greater importance has been accorded to economic issues; therefore any evaluation of Mercosur's successes and limitations must include both political and economic aspects.

From a political point of view Mercosur has achieved considerable results. The member states and five associates (Chile, Bolivia, Peru, Ecuador and Colombia) are all democracies, at least formally, despite enduring elements of social and political inequality. Mercosur played a decisive role in quashing General Oviedo's attempt at a *coup d'état* in Paraguay in 1996, and in 1998 the so-called 'democratic clause' was introduced stating that the presence of a democratic government was an essential condition for membership. Finally, Mercosur has presented itself both on the continent and internationally as a credible interlocutor, cohesive enough to increase the region's visibility and negotiating clout in global affairs. All the same, the one thing missing is widespread social participation in the Mercosur project. A subregional identity remains out of reach, and interest and support from civil society are at best intermittent.

Mercosur's record in the economic sector is mixed. The fact is that Mercosur has now existed for twenty years, but cannot yet be defined as a single market. Rather, it is a hybrid of a free trade area and an incomplete customs union. However, although this is evidently a limitation, the flexibility that accompanies this lack of definition has actually helped the bloc during periods of extreme crisis, such as in Brazil in 1997–99 and in Argentina in 2001/02. Undoubtedly the existence of a regional scheme reactivated the flow of foreign investment in the 1990s and generated a certain degree of economic modernization. Moreover, intra-area trade has tripled in less than a decade.[7] However, despite the stated intentions of the founding treaty, progress towards the free circulation of services, capital and labour has remained modest.

Based on this evidence, has Mercosur been a success or a failure? Looking at the state of affairs realistically and considering the conditions in which it began, Mercosur can be deemed a success, even though it raised many expectations (in fact somewhat excessive and often fed by hyperbolic rhetoric) which it has not achieved. As with all other regional aggregations, Mercosur's prospects for survival and improvement depend on two things: first, the sustainability of the project itself in terms of institutional deepening and membership enlargement; and secondly, domestic and international affairs.

The matter of institutional deepening, namely increasing the competencies and powers accorded to regional supranational bodies, has been a vital contributing factor to the success of the European Union. In Europe, the process of institutional development, although not always linear, has enjoyed the open support of the majority of member states, especially the most powerful ones. In Mercosur's case, there are various obstacles blocking the path towards further integration. In the current structure of Mercosur there is no equivalent body to the European Commission, a supranational organism with executive-type functions, independent and equipped with ample powers. This is due to the fact that since the very beginning member states (particularly the two biggest) favoured an intergovernmental approach to negotiations in order to maintain full control over the integration process. Social pressure for a European-style evolution is also virtually absent, as the business community and civil society are accustomed to discussing issues with their own national governments and look at the other member states with a certain degree of fear and scepticism.

There are also objective and structural obstacles to institutional consolidation. The creation of the Mercosur Parliament (Parlasur) offers an insightful example. The population of Brazil represents around 80 per cent of the total population of Mercosur countries. If Brazil were to be granted 80 per cent of the seats, this parliament would be devoid of any significance. On the other hand, options which deny Brazil a considerable degree of control over the institution would be very difficult for Brasilia to accept and would raise serious concerns over legitimacy. Contrary to the most pessimistic expectations, however, some progress has been made. In 2005 the four member countries had reached a compromise on a system of seat distribution whereby Brazil would not be allowed a majority, nor would the two smaller states have a right of veto, but the leadership of the two bigger states was confirmed and fortified and Brazil would be allowed to pursue its own agenda with the support of one single ally. This delicate situation meant that it was already unlikely the parliament would wield substantial powers, but the pending accession of Venezuela complicates negotiations still further and raises further questions over institutional consolidation agreements. The first universal and direct elections of the Parlasur were scheduled for 2011. At the time of writing no final agreement on the distribution of seats has been reached and the electoral exercise is likely to be postponed. Furthermore, even if significant agreements were approved for the further institutionalization of Mercosur, these would soon face additional difficulties, such as the search for resources to maintain an effective regional bureaucracy and the inclination of member states towards national autonomy in economic policy, critical for dealing with the recurrent economic and financial crises or to reap the gains of the current economic boom.

Enlargement is also an issue for Mercosur. During its first twenty years of existence it remained stable with the same four members which founded it in 1991. Venezuela's accession process remains peculiar. Caracas signed the accession protocol in 2006 but its ratification is still pending. In an ever more globalized world with increasingly intense multilateral negotiations, strategies that aim to build consensus and cohesion are certainly useful. However, these same strategies can also turn out to be highly problematic when it comes to political stability and economic cohesion within the bloc. The accession of Venezuela is an apt demonstration of such problems. The political stability of Chávez's Venezuela is difficult to verify. Although on the one hand its inclusion in Mercosur could tone down the dialectic and political excesses of Caracas, on the other hand Mercosur itself could suffer and even be damaged by it.

There are also objective obstacles impeding Mercosur's enlargement to include other countries in the region. Chile is the only neighbouring state with a stable and consolidated political system and a healthy economy. The current member states would be only too willing to welcome Santiago, but the reasons that saw the Chileans decline an invitation to join in 1991 are still valid: the common customs tariff theoretically in place for all Mercosur countries is higher than the customs barriers Chile imposes. It would be pointless for the country to compromise its own position on the world markets in exchange for presumably modest returns at a regional level. The free trade agreements that Chile, unlike Mercosur, has concluded with the United States and the European Union further complicate the situation. The ideological differences between Santiago and Caracas are another riddle to solve. At present, the accession of Bolivia, Peru, Ecuador and Colombia may similarly create more problems than benefits for Mercosur both politically and economically.

Mercosur, despite its ambiguities and contradictions, has thus far offered stability and progress to its member states. A process of enlargement in the future seems somewhat desirable to revitalize the project and ensure that it retains significance when faced with possible broader-ranging agreements, such as a hemispheric free trade area of some sort, a free trade agreement with the European Union or multilateral agreements within the World Trade Organization. In this respect, challenges may also come from other competing Latin American integration schemes such as UNASUR or CELAC, which are designed, among other things, to unify the region's positions on political and economic issues in multilateral forums. This point will be further discussed in the last section of this chapter.

The challenges of both possible enlargements and improved functioning must be shouldered at the political level. Only a Mercosur equipped with the appropriate bodies and resources will be able to act as a factor of regional growth and development and not a cause of stagnation or even collapse. This would, however, necessitate clear political will in favour of the Mercosur project as well as the widespread support and participation of civil society. Both seem to be in short supply at the moment. In the past the two biggest countries, Brazil and Argentina, have found the inspiration to make significant steps forward in the sphere of regional integration during difficult periods of profound international transformation.

Perhaps this, then, is the key to the future of Mercosur and Latin American integration.

NAFTA

Unlike Mercosur or the bilateral agreement between Argentina and Brazil, the North American Free Trade Agreement was not primarily conceived as an instrument to boost low levels of interaction between its member states (the USA, Mexico and Canada) but rather as a tool to manage the already extensive interdependence. Moreover, although it has of course made an impact on the economy, society and the environment, NAFTA has great political significance, being the first example of regional integration between northern and southern American countries with enormous cultural, never mind economic and political, differences.

Mexico's involvement in NAFTA raised questions about identity for the whole of Latin America, often defined as the antithesis of that northern giant, the United States. Mexico, one of its most populous states, has interlocked with Washington, and the consequences are significant not only for the economy but also for politics and identity. On the global political scene, Mexico seems to be moving away from the rest of the continent and drawing ever closer to its allied power. Mexican and US cultures seem to be mingling to create a new melting pot which distinguishes Mexico culturally from the rest of Latin America. An identity readjustment seems to be taking place not only in Mexico but throughout the region that describes itself as Latin America. Indeed, the very concept of Latin America seems to be under strain. Mexico and Central America, and to an extent the Caribbean archipelago, increasingly look north and model themselves politically and economically on the United States. South America, on the other hand, is distancing itself from Washington, its policies and even its values. The implications for Latin America in the twenty-first century may be substantial.

Like Mercosur and all of the other examples of Latin American integration, NAFTA too is the result of a process begun from the top, aspired to and pursued by governments, whereas their respective civil societies have been absent, tolerant or even opposed.

NAFTA is essentially the result of an evolution in Washington's policy towards its neighbours, particularly those in the South. Its conception represented the first step of a wider US plan for a new hemispheric order that seemed to take shape in the 1990s but was later frustrated at the beginning of the 2000s. As early as 1979, the United States announced that a North American free trade agreement had become a trade policy priority. The term 'North American', however, was not clarified at the time, but by the mid-1980s the US strategy regarding Mexico had become quite clear. In 1985 the USA and Mexico concluded a bilateral agreement on disputes over public subsidies, and in 1986 Mexico entered into the General Agreement on Tariffs and Trade (GATT), the precursor to the World Trade Organization (WTO). In 1987, a bilateral framework treaty was signed to liberalize trade and resolve potential disputes arising from it. In 1990, in an atmosphere of triumphant neoliberalism, Mexico officially requested that negotiations be opened on the creation of a free trade area, a project which the United States had already entered into two years previously with Canada. In 1992 the NAFTA constitutive treaty was signed, and it came into force in 1994. NAFTA is a much more detailed but much less ambitious economic integration scheme than Mercosur. There are no common or supranational structures, nor any aspiration to establish them. All negotiations take place on an exclusively intergovernmental basis.

Nonetheless, NAFTA's scope is much broader as it encompasses areas of competence much wider than mere trade liberalization, as its name would imply. NAFTA in fact covers not only trade issues but also regulates investment, promotes liberalization in the service sector, defines intellectual property rights and provides dispute resolution procedures for resolving differences which may arise in the areas covered by the treaty. While these measures may seem primarily economic, they call for a considerable degree of political cooperation and convergence. This is confirmed by the conclusion of several additional protocols pushed for by the Clinton presidency, such as the protocols regarding worker protection and cooperation in the environmental domain. Both of these topics are of major political and electoral interest, and civil society and pressure groups have been influential and have played a fundamental role, especially in the United States, and particularly in the anti-NAFTA camp.

Both protocols were negotiated by the Clinton administration to tame the potentially negative effects – in fact quite negligible in comparison to the benefits – that the treaty could have had on important US constituencies. Although the dominant role of the United States within NAFTA is accepted and understandable, it is also important to consider what advantages other member states gain by joining the treaty.

Clearly, there are both economic and political advantages for the USA, but one might ask why it did not pursue these objectives unilaterally by playing on its own political and economic influence without committing to a treaty. To understand this it is imperative to remember the precise historical context in which NAFTA was concluded. At the beginning of the 1990s, enthusiasm following the end of the Cold War was accompanied by a mounting perception that countries were positioning themselves to participate in global competition by forming regional blocs. In the United States there were fears of Europe as a thriving but hardly accessible single market and an aggressive trader. Also, perceptions of a flourishing and competitive Japan were combined with disillusionment over the modest results of GATT's attempts to discipline world trade. This led to renewed interest in Mexico as a potential ally for forming a North American trading bloc. Moreover, the existing interdependence at the border between Mexico and the United States in areas such as environmental pollution, drug trafficking and illegal immigration was a clear sign to Washington that these challenges could not be confronted unilaterally. Instead, the other countries involved would need to cooperate. This prompted the final and decisive push towards the regionalism option.

Mexico's accession to NAFTA signalled a distinct break from traditional Mexican foreign policy, until then geared towards maintaining the nation's political and economic autonomy from its powerful neighbour. Furthermore, Mexico had been wary of closer commercial ties with the United States for years owing to fears over the costs of adaptation, particularly to employment in the agricultural and manufacturing sectors. The catastrophic economic crisis in 1982, the failure of industrialization through import substitution, the need to maintain privileged access to the US market as well as the arrival of President Salinas and his neoliberal leanings compelled the Mexican ruling elite to review their positions. When Mexico joined NAFTA it gained guaranteed, regular access to the US market and a legal and institutional framework for limiting North American unilateral tendencies. It also became more attractive to foreign investors. However, many of the issues for which NAFTA was conceived remained unsolved. To this day, Mexico is a key transit country for drugs en route to the USA. Illegal immigration of desperate populations from Central and South America across the Mexican border is ceaseless. The environmental discipline imposed by NAFTA has reduced ecological problems only in the industrial zone at the border, while social legislation, in spite of the improvements it has made to working conditions in Mexico, has benefited local development precious little.

The future of NAFTA seems more closely connected to the ambitions of its most powerful member than to any situations or occurrences within the integration scheme. NAFTA did not set out to enlarge as such by allowing new members to join its treaty. It has no ambition to deepen institutional coordination but represents a model for cooperation policy and for the Latin American and continental order that Washington seems to have in mind. In this way, the United States prepared a strategy for expanding the NAFTA model, including the conclusion of free trade agreements with other Central and South American countries in view of the establishment of the Free Trade Area of the Americas (FTAA), which aims to create a gigantic free trade area from Alaska to Tierra del Fuego.

The FTAA project collapsed in 2005 when at the Mar del Plata summit Latin American countries rejected it. This was not for its principles but for its contents, perceived as very beneficial to the USA and of very little benefit to the rest of the Americas. Also, attempts recently conducted by the Obama administration to revive the plan have so far been ineffective. The USA has thus reverted to a bilateral approach, signing FTA agreements modelled on NAFTA with several South American countries and with Central America and the Dominican Republic (DR-CAFTA). This network of individual and subregional FTAs is meant to increase the price of exclusion for states that decide not to sign. But on the one hand those which have not signed yet are the most powerful and less dependent South American states, such as Brazil; on the other hand, alternative regional options and international partners are now available to Latin America, which underlines the limits of the US approach to continental trade.

The main constraint of this approach is the highly unbalanced relationship between the United States and the rest of the continent, meaning that the creation of such a network of agreements is essentially dependent on the will of one single party. What's more, the interests of the United States in Latin America cover only certain sectors and do not have the same impact on the whole of the continent. Levels of interdependence with many South American states are rather low. In addition, Washington has no interest in any continental agreement which would be exclusive or take priority over trade relations between the USA and other parts of the world, or trade partners that are much more important for the US economy, such as the European Union and increasingly China. Finally, US public opinion does not harbour particularly positive attitudes towards these agreements, and their hypothetical ratification in the Senate could generate further problems, including electoral ones which no US president would want to confront.

In summary, the USA is lacking the strong desire and political will to bond with the rest of the American continent. It perceives the regionalism strategy as a way to pursue its own objectives on the continent while retaining a wide degree of autonomy. Latin Americans, on the other hand, would be favourable to a more institutionalized system which would protect their interests in other areas of little importance to the USA. These remarks seem to apply to all of the examples of regionalism to which the United States belongs, including NAFTA, the network of free trade agreements, and further elaboration of the inter-American system or future, although now unlikely, Free Trade Agreement of the Americas.

The Andean Community

Mercosur is the most important truly Latin American subregional integration scheme, and NAFTA is the most interesting and, thus far, unique example of integration between countries of North and Latin

America. However, during the 1990s a series of other agreements were revived or conceived in other areas of Latin America, and of these the Andean Community perhaps best embodies the efforts, difficulties and contradictions of contemporary Latin American regionalism.

The Andean Community (Comunidad Andina, CAN) has progressed in an unusual manner: although some institutional developments have been made, these have not been accompanied by similar increases in political sway or economic-commercial growth. Crucially, cohesion has always been problematic within the bloc. In the 1970s Chile left the Community and Venezuela joined. During the same decade, agreements were endorsed for the creation of a Court of Justice, an Andean Parliament and an Andean Council of Foreign Ministers. The impact of this institutional effort has, however, been modest both on the national politics of member states and the negotiating weight of the Community as a whole at the international level. After slipping almost into inactivity in the 1980s, the Community was relaunched at the start of the 1990s with the arrival of the new neoliberal paradigm. Between 1990 and 1991, the CAN made the decision to accelerate the process for the formation of an Andean free trade area and adopt a common external customs tariff, which came into force in 1995. In 1998 the bloc had its first successes as a unified entity in negotiations. The Andean Community spoke with one voice on behalf of member states in negotiations over the creation of a Free Trade Area of the Americas, and a framework agreement for the establishment of a free trade area between the Community and Mercosur was signed. In the same year, following peace treaties to resolve territorial disputes between Ecuador and Peru, the latter was gradually integrated into the Community's free trade area. The following year, the Community decided to establish an Andean common market by 2005. Despite these numerous advances, the economic and social situation in Andean countries has improved little, and the role of the bloc in these improvements has been marginal. The Community's international clout remains limited too. The recent association of Argentina, Brazil, Chile, Uruguay and Paraguay will not change the situation greatly; the common market is still a chimera and many of the standards approved at a

Community level are notable for their exceptions, partial application and complicated overlaps with other agreements between member states or between members and other nearby countries.

However, the lack of cohesion between members of the bloc and of a clear and steady direction are the main factors which put the development and even the survival of the Community at risk. While Chile rejoined in 2006 as an associate member, Venezuela decided to leave the CAN in the same year in order to participate in Mercosur. The two choices seem to be two sides of the same coin. Although on the one hand joining the CAN brings useful commercial benefits, when it comes to political and strategic choices there are better options for embarking upon Latin American regionalism. That explains why Chile chose associated member status (as it has also done in Mercosur), giving it access to economic advantages but in practice falling short of any political commitment. Venezuela, conversely, was looking for allies for its own political plan of international insertion and a profound rethink of regional integration schemes, and has evidently chosen the partners it deems strongest and most credible on the international scene. Also, the 2008 bombing of Ecuadorean territory by Colombia in the pursuit of guerrilla terrorists cast serious doubts on the political relevance of the Community. It would be unthinkable for any member of the EU, for instance, to conduct military operations in another member state to chase criminals.

A worry for the CAN is the Community's potential loss of meaning with the signature of bilateral free trade agreements between Peru, Ecuador, Colombia and the United States, which the Washington Senate is now expected to ratify. If these agreements entered into force and North American goods gained free access to the three Andean signatory countries, the CAN standards concerning common external customs tariffs, along with efforts to construct a common Andean market, could be deprived of all meaning. On the other hand, the three countries are largely dependent on Washington for their exports and incoming capital flows. When faced with a choice between guaranteed regular access to the US market and the pursuance of an autonomous political and regional project with a low immediate economic return, Peru and Colombia plumped for the first option. President Correa of Ecuador, on the other hand, denounced the agreement and pursued a rapprochement with Chávez's Venezuela. To complicate things further, Morales in Bolivia has adopted a stance similar to that of Chávez. In 2006 he explicitly invited the three partners to withdraw from the agreement with Washington, intensifying tensions within the bloc. Although theoretically speaking strong economic bonds with the North and the attempt to reinforce the political weight of the Community or the Latin American macro-area are not incompatible, in practical terms this combination is likely to be untenable. It would deprive the CAN of much of its already limited economic significance, would raise concern among Mercosur associated partners, who have so far rejected an FTA with the USA, and would increase frictions within the bloc. Most worrying, such a step may make the CAN irrelevant to the development strategies of its members, more and more oriented towards the Chinese, Asian and the US markets.

The Andean Community thus exemplifies existing tensions between political aspirations to unite and reform the Latin American world and dependence on the US market, or increasingly the Chinese market. Currently and for the immediate future, the only solution seems to be steady pragmatism which would allow Latin American countries to understand each other's reasoning and weaknesses and lead to lasting agreements on a limited range of topics as the lowest common denominator. Sadly, the 2008 diplomatic crisis between Ecuador, Colombia and Venezuela following Colombian anti-terrorist operations on Ecuadorean soil revealed just how little the Andean Community counts when political stakes are high and how far there is to go in terms of political coordination, let alone economic coordination, in the CAN.

The inter-American system

One of the most interesting forms of regionalism involving Latin American countries is the so-called inter-American system, a set of political, economic and human rights institutions at the continental level which, although they have been in place since the immediate aftermath of the Second World War, were given a new lease of life during the 1990s. The Organization of American States (OAS) is the mainstay of this system. Founded after the Second World War to promote coordination and dialogue between the states of the American continent, it evolved into an instrument for protecting US interests throughout the Cold War. For example, Cuba was expelled from the OAS under US pressure following attempts to instal Soviet nuclear missiles on the island in 1962, and is still excluded from the work of the Organization for political reasons to this day. Thus emptied of its initial *raison d'être*, the OAS survived in a state of near-immobility until the 1990s. With the fall of communism and the need to promote democracy in Latin America, the OAS was revitalized and found a purpose in defending democracy within the framework of inter-American institutions.

In 1991 the OAS member countries signed the so-called Santiago Commitment, promoting human rights and representative democracy. Resolution 1080 gave the OAS new powers and means to act. The resolution stated that if democracy were interrupted or unexpectedly endangered in one of the member states, the foreign affairs ministers of the signatory countries were bound to call a meeting within ten days to analyse the situation. This procedure was a complete change from the past, when national sovereignty was considered inviolable and processes of internal political organization were the remit of national authorities alone. With Resolution 1080, domestic circumstances became a sufficient reason for the Organization to intervene in the internal affairs of a member state. The OAS foreign affairs ministers could even collectively adopt decisions and measures which they judge suitable for re-establishing the interrupted democratic order. What's more, the 1992 Washington Protocol amended the OAS Founding Charter, giving the General Assembly of member states powers to suspend, by a two-thirds majority vote, states whose governments had come to power through a *coup d'état* or in any other way by illegally divesting a democratically elected government of authority. The commitment to democracy was further reinforced with the Managua Declaration in 1993, decreeing that member states were bound to pursue democracy as their aim and to bolster their own democratic institutions, and protect human rights and the rights of minorities.

Moreover, the Organization has been supported in its actions and defence of democracy since 1990 by the Unit for the Promotion of Democracy, an OAS department which conducts studies and research and provides information and staff training to member states which request it to facilitate the consolidation of democratic institutions. The Unit has been a success, promoting itself as a credible tool for electoral monitoring, providing observers to guarantee the regularity of elections in many Latin American countries and providing technical assistance to countries which require it to create modern and efficient electoral laws. Unfortunately, the Unit is a somewhat isolated case as other new provisions of the OAS have met with insurmountable problems when it came to their implementation.

Looking back at how Resolution 1080 has been applied, it becomes clear that without an effective display of will and resources on the part of member states these powers simply ring hollow. This problem is common to many international organizations, not least the United Nations. Between 1991 and 1994, for example, the democratic government of Haiti was ousted by a military coup. Despite OAS measures permitted by Resolution 1080, democratic order could be restored only when US troops intervened under a UN mandate. When the *autogolpe* or self-coup occurred in Peru in 1992, with the democratically elected President Fujimori interrupting the democratic order to increase his own powers and control over the state, the actions of the OAS had only a negligible practical effect, and its limited influence produced just a slight tensing of economic relations with the United States. The attempted coup in Paraguay in 1996 was thwarted more because of pressure applied by members of Mercosur than because of OAS intervention. The Organization's dependency on US funds and political benevolence made interventions more problematic. Even the fleeting burst of life in the 1990s does not seem to have supplied enough momentum for the new millennium, and Latin America's sense of ownership of the organization remains rather limited. The creation of UNASUR and the CELAC project (see next section) may further weaken OAS reach and scope in the protection of hemispheric security and democracy.

The OAS has also created the inter-American human rights system, a quite complex mechanism that is made up of four elements:

1 The American Declaration of the Rights and Duties of Man;
2 The American Convention on Human Rights;
3 The Inter-American Commission on Human Rights;
4 The Inter-American Court of Human Rights.

The American Declaration of the Rights and Duties of Man (1948) shares many of the principles espoused by the Universal Declaration of Human Rights, adopted a few months later as another response to the terrible events of the Second World War. The American Declaration is not legally binding, nor is it intended to be; nonetheless, it is in a way indirectly binding through the Founding Charter of the OAS, which is binding for member states and refers explicitly to the protection of human rights as defined by the aforementioned declaration. This is significant because some OAS member states did not sign the 1969 American Convention on Human Rights (namely the United States and Canada in addition to Cuba). Thus the only obligations for these states are those emanating from the Declaration through the references to it incorporated in the Founding Charter of the OAS.

The American Convention on Human Rights is a treaty between states. Unlike the International Covenant on Civil and Political Rights of the UN, the American Convention deals with property rights, at the request of the USA, and more exhaustively covers citizens' rights to participate in the political affairs, particularly in government, of their own country. The states that adhere to the Convention commit on the one hand to respecting the rights and liberties recognized by the Convention and on the other hand to pursuing the principle of non-discrimination with regard to race, gender, colour, language, religion and political opinions. The Convention applies to all human beings (but not companies, trade unions, cooperatives, etc.) and to every person under the jurisdiction of one of the signatories. Dispensations are permitted only in the case of true emergencies such as war, public danger or other threats to security or the independence of a contracting party.

The Inter-American Commission on Human Rights was established by an OAS resolution and commenced operations in 1960. The Commission is made up of seven independent members nominated by OAS member states and elected by the OAS General Assembly. The Commission is a semi-permanent body which meets for eight weeks per year in Washington. It can arrange hearings and carry out site visits, but its conclusions and recommendations are not binding for states. Nevertheless, the examination of individual petitions is becoming increasingly important. The Commission's role and operations have been criticized, however, owing mainly to the alleged lack of admissibility checks, attempts by states to apply pressure to influence case proceedings, and a lack of coherence in the treatment of cases depending on their political significance and the power of the states under investigation. Some problems, especially the congestion issue, could be resolved by increasing the budget, but member states are somewhat reluctant to finance an institution which has the power to criticize them.

Finally, the Inter-American Court of Human Rights is also a semi-permanent body with its headquarters in San José, the capital of Costa Rica. The Court is made up of seven independent judges, nominated by states that participate in the Convention and elected by the same small group of states but under the aegis of the OAS General Assembly. The Court is an exclusively judicial body. It can provide opinions on the interpretation of the Convention and the other human rights treaties in the Americas and pass judgments on controversial cases referred to it by the Commission or by a member state of the Convention. The judgments of the Court are binding but can be made only with regard to certain states which, as well as being members of the Convention, have also explicitly signed a special optional declaration accepting the Court's jurisdiction. Unsurprisingly, until recently the Court's activity has been extremely limited, both because of the low number of states that have signed the optional declaration, and the Commission's reluctance to act against member states.

The inter-American system for protecting human rights is a positive addition to instruments of cooperation at the continental level; nonetheless, it is faced with significant limitations and several contradictions which appear paradoxical but at the same time are perhaps inevitable. The Commission and the Court have jurisdiction only over states that signed the 1969 Convention. The fact that this does not include the United States undermines the continental aspect of the system and undermines its credibility. For historic and other reasons, the system has almost exclusively dealt with grave violations, such as firing squads, torture, state homicides and arbitrary detention, thus neglecting out of necessity the everyday situation regarding human rights in member states. Like all other international organizations that deal with human rights, the inter-American system also has a dilemma: it was founded and is funded by members (states) over which it should exercise control. The states confer significant powers to the system but in reality they retain control over its functioning by electing its members, allocating resources, enforcing decisions and, perhaps most importantly, completing preparatory work and drafting the agenda. In other words, the controlled have ample power to determine the scope and nature of the actions of the controller.

The inter-American system is completed by its economic arm, the Inter-American Development Bank (IADB or Banco Interamericano de Desarrollo, BID), founded in 1959 as a driver of technical and financial development and an intellectual stimulus for growth in the region. The Bank began with twenty Latin American countries and the United States, and included Cuba in initial proceedings, although it did not accede. Its foundation occurred after a wave of renewed US interest in Latin American economic development with a view to rendering the continent impenetrable to Soviet influence during the Cold War, but the activity and priorities of the IADB have evolved significantly over the past few decades.

In the 1960s, developing countries participated in the rapid expansion of the world economy but struggled to access capital. The IADB focused on this aspect of primary importance, financing loans to states in need of works and infrastructure in the construction sector, health, education, higher education and regional integration. This was perfectly consistent with the dominant stance of the time, i.e. development stimulated by public capital and the involvement of the state, according to the theories of ECLAC. At the time, the United States was the only member country which was a net contributor.

During the 1970s, the IADB tried to attract new resources. Canada was the first state defined as non-regional to be admitted as a member without rights to loans. Other industrialized countries were invited to join in this capacity, and between 1976 and 1978 fifteen countries accepted the invitation. The two oil crises of 1974 and 1979 and Latin America's accumulation of colossal debts to private banks saw the Bank's role gradually diminish.

The 1980s were a period of intense crisis both for Latin American countries and for the IADB. The debt crisis resulted in a negative net transfer of financial resources out of Latin America, and the Bank had to readjust its priorities and its institutional role. The main area of activity was no longer support for development but interventions to guarantee the very financial survival of certain countries, and many programmes moved from supporting the public sector to immediate interventions to shore up the disaster-struck balance of payments of several Latin American countries.

The IADB was also affected by the sea-changes of the 1990s. The advent of neoliberalism with its economic formulas, such as trade liberalization and privatization, and the injection of new private capital flows resulted in a slight improvement in the economic and financial conditions of the poorest members and further redefinition of the role of the Bank. It now focused on assisting interested countries in introducing much-needed fiscal reforms and liberalizing commercial policy. The role of the Bank also benefited from renewed enthusiasm and consensus in favour of inter-American institutions, typical of the early 1990s. The IADB supported US plans to create a Free Trade Area of the Americas and actively endeavoured to promote private investment in Latin America. To this end, the Multilateral Investment Fund was set up and run by the Bank to provide technical assistance and financial support for launching private companies and for building up and training human resources.

Since the turn of the century the Inter-American Development Bank has tried to keep in step with the new demands and trends of its Latin American members, tempering its orthodox neoliberal precepts and paying closer attention to social development and human capital. This is reflected in the IADB's new priorities, now centred on redistributive policies, reducing poverty, social reforms, infrastructure and good governance of public affairs (fighting corruption, administrative efficiency and transparency, responsibility and accountability in public administration, and guaranteeing the application of the law).

In summary, of all the institutions that are part of the inter-American system the Inter-American Development Bank has adapted most successfully to the contemporary situation by serving its most needy members. The Bank pays special attention to developing countries, especially the poorest ones, on which it confers the special status of member countries with rights to loans. Traditionally, these countries have held the majority of votes within the decision-making bodies of the organization, conferring on Latin American countries a sense of ownership and belonging to the system. This sentiment is felt to be lacking in other institutions of the inter-American system, such as the OAS. Even now, the percentage of votes held by IADB member states with a right to loans cannot be less than 50 per cent of the total number. Although there are unavoidable weaknesses, most of the per capita resources have been given to the smallest and poorest countries, and today's priorities appear to be in line with the current situation and the demands voiced directly by the community of Latin American countries.

Latin American regionalism in the new millennium

As the neoliberal model began to be questioned, considerable effects were felt both at the national and the regional level. Nationally, many governments now implement policies with a greater focus on social development and the lives of their citizens. Regionally, as a direct consequence of domestic developments, new models have been launched to reflect these priorities and provide alternatives to the traditional regionalist projects that are largely the product of the neoliberal experience. Latin American countries now seem to be at the stage of reconsidering their models for regionalism, inspired by four driving principles:

1 Moving on from, or evolving, the neoliberal model in favour of a model which promotes sustainable development as opposed to macroeconomic orthodoxy and mere economic growth.
2 Learning constructive lessons from the mistakes of the past, in particular avoiding overly ambitious undertakings in favour of a

more realistic and feasible approach proportionate to available resources.

3 Building a unique path to regionalism which does not imitate imported models, but instead is based on the real needs of the region together with its culture and tradition.
4 Pragmatism and openness towards all potential international partners. This includes a critical examination of the region's position within international organizations as well as strategic and commercial alliances.

At the hemispheric level, there seems to be a diminution of interest in a Free Trade Area of the Americas (FTAA). Indeed, the continent seems to be splitting between a northern part (from Alaska to the Panama Canal, and including the Caribbean) that hinges around the United States, and because of choice or necessity aligns itself with Washington, and a southern part, comprising South America, that broadly seeks more autonomy from the USA and proposes new regional formulas and organizations to pursue an independent and effective incorporation in the global scenario. At present, the FTAA project has lost momentum.

The FTAA idea owes much to the climate of enthusiasm and cooperation that underpinned the resurrection of pan-Americanism in the early 1990s. The FTAA project took shape with the launch of the Enterprise for the Americas by US president George Bush senior in 1990, later pushed forward by the Clinton presidency. In 1994, the First Summit of the Americas, which gathered heads of state and government from all of the countries on the continent, with the exception of Cuba, which is still being boycotted by the United States, agreed that negotiations on the FTAA would be finalized by 2005. However, at the 2005 Fourth Summit of the Americas in Mar del Plata (Argentina) strong resistance to the project emerged on the Latin American side. The deadline passed without any significant agreement being reached and the political and economic climate of the 1990s has completely changed in the new millennium.

The USA is no longer the only model available or the global and continental hegemon. In the 2000s, the USA was increasingly criticized in Latin America and its neoliberal economic solutions revised and adapted to Latin American local needs and interests. The United States itself appears to have lost enthusiasm for the FTAA format and seems to be reverting to the bilateral agreements strategy. The Mercosur countries also seem somewhat reluctant to accept the terms outlined by the United States for the FTAA and have proposed their own agenda for negotiations. Furthermore, Brazil, one of the FTAA's primary opponents, is an emerging power and seems able to gather enough consensus in the region to pursue alternative routes. Since the 2000s neoliberal presidents in Latin America have been replaced by more progressive administrations, often outspoken critics of the North American model. If an Americas-wide trade agreement could be reached at all, it is more likely to take the shape of a network of smaller agreements rather than one large and comprehensive deal.

Yet some advocate the relaunch of the FTAA negotiations in the wake of very recent developments. The rise of Brazil to international power status and the growth of China's influence in Latin America may provide both the USA and up to now reluctant Latin American countries enough incentive to conclude some sort of preferential trade deal. It is not a coincidence, for instance, that the difficulty of achieving a multilateral agreement within the WTO has induced many Latin American countries to look benignly on the possible relaunching of the FTAA. This relaunch process, which should have been initiated at the Fifth Summit of the Americas in Trinidad and Tobago in April 2009, has yielded few visible results.

At the Latin American continental level, changes and innovative aggregations are emerging. South America is rising as a geopolitical unit of its own. Many South American administrations are distancing themselves from the North. They have opted for a compelling quest for a more autonomous and multipolar international and regional order. The creation of the South American Union (UNASUR), which comprises all twelve South American countries, is the result of Brazil's vision to constitute 'South America' as a cohesive and politically active community.

The notion of a South American common space has a long history but its political and economic construction is much more recent, and was given significant momentum and a more political content by President Cardoso of Brazil during the First South American Summit in 2000. The 2004 Cuzco summit created the Community of South American Nations (CSN), which marked the launch of a South American political project, while the 2008 Treaty of Brasilia established UNASUR. In principle, UNASUR represents the world's fifth economic bloc with an annual combined GDP of US$2.915 trillion and a total population of over 380 million people. The strengths of UNASUR may well simultaneously prove to be weaknesses. First, the fact that it is the product of a Brazilian initiative provides the bloc with a designated, or self-designated, leader, with an obvious interest in a return from the success of the organization. At the same time, Brazilian preponderance generates resistance and makes the success of the group over-dependent on Brazil's own domestic and international preferences. Secondly, the fact that UNASUR claims to represent a new regional entity, South America (as opposed to Latin America), on the one hand, makes the grouping geographically well defined and geostrategically less elusive, but on the other leaves to one side a player like Mexico, whose trade and cultural importance to the region should not be underestimated. Thirdly, the fact that all twelve South American countries joined the group may give it a certain legitimacy and weight, but also creates problems of coordination and compatibility given the variety and heterogeneity of the members' political and economic positions and agendas.

Born as a quite pragmatic and focused project under the label of the Community of South American States, UNASUR has become increasingly wide ranging and expressly political in nature. The intention of limiting US influence in South America by proposing itself as a counter-actor to the OAS in regional security matters, coupled with ambitious goals in the area of employment, education, health and fighting poverty, runs the risk of making the venture over-ambitious. In particular, the aspiration to an institutional structure based on the model of the European Union, including the creation of a parliament, a single currency, a Bank of the South and a common passport, may seriously affect the ability of member states to realize the initiative. It does not seem to take into proper account the geographical, demographic, economic, political and unique historical circumstances that made the European Union the way it is today. Also, doubts exist about the real political will and economic capacity of all members to support the project. If UNASUR were successful and became fully functioning by 2019, as its proponents hope, this would have a strong impact on the equilibrium of the American continent and perhaps beyond.

A first challenge to UNASUR is already materializing with the project of a Community of Latin American and Caribbean States (Comunidad de Estados Latinoamericanos y del Carribe – CELAC). CELAC would include all the American states except the USA and Canada, thus reviving the concept of Latin America and constituting a Latin American political bloc to increase negotiating weight at the global level. Its beginnings have been less than promising, however. The July 2011 summit that should have marked the formal constitution of the bloc was called off because of President Chávez's illness. It is at the very least peculiar that an international summit of such supposed magnitude should be postponed because one head of state cannot attend. While it is premature to offer any assessment of the project, it certainly has the potential to change the regional and international scenario considerably. Alternatively, it might also confirm the historical inability of Latin American countries to stick together when the stakes are high.

At the subregional level too significant innovations have taken place in order to reflect in regional projects the new lines adopted by the pink tide administrations, and not only domestically. The best example is perhaps the Bolivarian Alliance for the Americas (Alianza Bolivariana para las Américas, ALBA), initiated by Venezuelan president Hugo Chávez. According to Chávez's vision, the major obstacle to Latin American development is the poverty and social inequality typical of the subcontinent. Consequently, a vital first step is to increase the living standards of the population through endogenous (from within) development. Simply put, this is a territory's capacity to model its own future from within and recognize three key issues: cultural specificity, entrepreneurial potential and the efficiency of local institutions. The first application of ALBA's principles materialized with the Venezuelan–Cuban agreement of 2004, while Bolivia, under the presidency of Evo Morales, joined in 2006. At present, Venezuela, Cuba, Nicaragua, Dominica, Ecuador,

San Vicente and the Grenadines, and Antigua and Barbuda are full members of ALBA.

ALBA associates are inspired by the Bolivarian ideals of Latin American political unity, solidarity and endogenous development, but these principles remain loosely codified or institutionalized. It is also primarily a political project and is ruled by the pre-eminence of the political over the economic. Its key objectives are the fight against poverty and the pursuit of social development, and it was in fact created as a reaction against neoliberal economics and as an alternative to the existing and proposed integration schemes based on neoliberal foundations. It opposed the US-sponsored Free Trade Area of the Americas (FTAA), and also opposes those Latin American integration schemes, such as Mercosur and the Andean Community, which share the US preference for free trade, privatization and deregulation. The result is a strongly ideological vision. On the one hand, only those countries strictly adhering to the Bolivarian ideology are welcome to join, while on the other a confrontational stance towards those not sharing these principles is almost inevitable given the importance of the issues at stake, the rigidity of positions and the inflammatory rhetoric. This means that the grouping is not attractive to a majority of Latin American countries; it is also potentially divisive as it exacerbates the dichotomy between supporters and non-supporters of the project.

Under the current circumstances it seems unlikely that this radical alternative will become a lasting and sustainable project. ALBA is a unilateral proposal made by the Venezuelan government and highly dependent on the will and mood of President Chávez. Its resources, although contributed by members depending on their capacity, are highly reliant on Venezuelan oil and generosity linked to ideological affinities. The involvement of the social parties, a key aim of the organization, remains limited in terms of policy design. Support for this strategy in Latin America is rather feeble. Furthermore, Venezuela's participation in other regional projects such as UNASUR, CELAC and possibly Mercosur will demand a reconsideration of the nature and purpose of ALBA. Additional contradictions and complexities emerge when one considers that Nicaragua is at the same time a member of ALBA and DR-CAFTA, and that Ecuador enjoys free access to the US market for most of its products within the US Andean Trade Promotion and Drug Eradication Act, for the renewal of which it has actively campaigned while formally acceding to ALBA and denouncing the FTA with the USA. More than anything else, the fate of the organization seems tied to that of Hugo Chávez. Rather than offering a comprehensive regional alternative, ALBA could end up acting as a supplement to other, more pragmatic initiatives.

Mercosur too has evolved according to changes in the national agenda and priorities of member states. At the beginning of the 2000s Mercosur had lost impetus owing to the failures of the neoliberal model upon which it had been designed and the economic crisis in Brazil and Argentina that led the two bigger members to disregard many of their regional commitments. From 2003 onwards Mercosur started a new phase, seeking to rebalance politics and economics to achieve effective economic and social development at the same time. The need to generate a new negotiating impetus was affirmed at the 2003 presidential summit in Asunción – the first attended by left-leaning Lula of Brazil and Kirchner of Argentina – where a number of proposals were also discussed to give a new focus to the integration project. Brazil presented its proposal *Objetivo 2006* to relaunch the creation of the customs union and the pursuit of the political and social dimensions of Mercosur. Argentina proposed the creation of a Mercosur Monetary Institute to diminish the bloc's dependence on international financial institutions. Paraguay stressed the need to address the asymmetries between larger and smaller members. Although these plans have achieved limited practical results, thus confirming the gap between intentions and deeds, they have contributed to changing the approach to regional integration and prompted an adjustment of the Mercosur agenda.

The definite intellectual shift from the previous neoliberal phase took place when Presidents Kirchner and Lula signed a document called *Consenso de Buenos Aires*, which marked a clear departure, at least in conceptual terms, from the Washington Consensus of the 1990s. The document affirmed the right of people to development and the centrality of the state in public policy, and stressed the values of integration as well as the need for the participation of civil society. Since 2004 social issues have appeared on the Mercosur agenda, with initiatives such as Somos Mercosur, the organization of Mercosur summits of social actors, and the creation of a Social Institute of Mercosur. Also, more traditional issues gained new momentum, with the entry into force of the Olivos Protocol establishing a Permanent Tribunal of Revision in 2004, the creation of a Structural Convergence Fund (FOCEM) in 2004 to tackle asymmetries between bigger and smaller members, and the opening of Parlasur in 2006. This reflects a change of attitude, priorities and policy at the national and regional levels. The political and social dimensions now better complement the economic side of Mercosur.

Conclusions

The new priorities brought in by the progressive administrations and the changed international circumstances have found a prompt response at the regional level in Latin America. If one considers the lengthy negotiations that characterize politics and institutional transformation, Latin America has been quite swift. The intergovernmental logic, and the absence of truly supranational bodies, amplifies responsiveness at the regional level to national political preferences over time. Yet the gap between discourse and good intentions on the one hand and reality and implementation on the ground on the other persists. This confirms not only the tension between discourse and practice but also those between unity and diversity and change and continuity that equally characterize Latin American regionalism, as well as the analytical framework of this book.

Under the current formulations and formats, Latin American regionalism, although meant to be an expression of unity and solidarity, has become a stark reflection of diversity and heterogeneity. Even in the presence of supposedly ideological affinities between a majority of the current progressive administrations, Latin America is characterized by a number of competing regional projects, whose rationales and agendas are often divergent, if not incompatible. Yet the quest for regional unity remains strong, and the vitality and variety of old and new projects are better understood from this perspective.

More generally, although there is a Latin American identity, it is defined mainly by what Latin America is 'not' (essentially the USA). What's more, Latin American identity is being constantly challenged and remodelled by globalization and the diffusion of a common model of aspirations and behaviours: the Western model. However, this is accompanied by a parallel surge in genuinely local Latin American customs and traditions. So, for example, Bolivian-style handicrafts have now reached the street markets of Chile and similar objects can be found in Central America too. These are processes that affect the entire world; this is part of globalization. The so-called pink tide is trying to combine international insertion with independence and respect for localness. This is probably a global trend whereby the local and the global try to find ways to coexist. The place of regionalism might be found in between these two tendencies, in Latin America and beyond. As Barry Buzan suggests, the world of tomorrow may be characterized by relatively autonomous regional aggregations interconnected through global networks.[8]

THREE
Latin America in the world: between change and continuity

Introduction

Latin America's position in the twenty-first-century world shows both elements of continuity and signs of change from the past. High dependence on international markets is an element of continuity and the recent 'reprimarization' of many Latin American economies with the boom in commodities and foodstuff exports to Asia is likely not to change this feature but to reinforce it. The significant presence of the United States, albeit diminishing or simply evolving, is another main element of continuity compared to the past, and so is the Latin American quest for alternatives and counterbalances to US influence in politics, the economy and culture. Following internal transformations in Latin American countries from the 1990s onwards, the seesaw of rhetoric and pragmatism has also often been reflected in the international image of the continent. In fact, perhaps one of the most novel elements is the apparent surge of renewed pragmatism in international relations. This is impelling Latin American countries to reconsider principles and paradigms which are for the most part imported from elsewhere in the world, to evaluate foreign policy positions closely and with a long-term perspective, and to seek negotiated solutions and avoid open conflict either with heavyweight Northern neighbours or other possible political or trade partners, with a special focus on South–South cooperation. For historic and geostrategic reasons, this chapter pays particular attention to the current status of relations between Latin America and the United States, before analysing relations with the European Union and the ascent of Chinese influence.

Relations with the United States: from the historical and philosophical roots to the end of the twentieth century

In order to understand the evolution of the relationship between the North and South of the American continent over time, and to appreciate the breadth of current changes, it is important to consider some objective facts and the philosophical stamp both sides have imprinted on this relationship from the beginning. The United States is now, and has been since the end of the Second World War, the single major political, economic, military and cultural power at the world level, challenged only by the Soviet Union during the Cold War and perhaps by China in the future. On the American continent, the USA had become the dominant actor as early as the nineteenth century, then along with Great Britain. While the United States was hurtling towards rapid industrialization and advances in the domestic market in the 1800s, Latin American countries were still wrestling with political and territorial consolidation in the post-independence years and struggling with the colonial legacy of an economy with primitive structures and centred on exports of goods, particularly raw materials and agricultural produce, to international markets. This engendered a structural imbalance: on the one hand, a country with strong political structures and an economy growing exponentially and on the other hand a group of separate countries with weak political bases and mostly struggling economies highly dependent on trade relations with the bigger powers of the time.

This situation, already asymmetric from an objective point of view, was exacerbated by different perceptions of themselves and their mutual relations. The United States was a self-confident young nation that perceived itself as unique, blessed by God and destined to greatness. The USA coloured its international position with philosophical statements intending to justify and reinforce its leading role in the hemisphere. Latin American countries, as a reaction, assumed a defensive posture and tried to have recourse to international law and Latin American unity to limit US interference and expansion. In 1823, US president Monroe had pronounced his doctrine stating that the American continent should not be considered a future target for colonization by Europe. The Monroe Doctrine revealed a fundamental aspect of Washington's policy towards Latin America:

keeping other big powers out of an area perceived as belonging to its sphere of influence. Although the Monroe Doctrine was a warning to Europe, it was not, however, to be interpreted as an attack on the principle of colonialism, but rather as a limitation to European expansionism in the Americas to allow space for increased US influence. The 1896 Olney Corollary (Olney was the US Secretary of State at the time) unilaterally declared US predominance in the American hemisphere, putting an end to Britain's claims and role. The circle was tightened via the corollary announced by President Theodore Roosevelt in 1904, affirming that the USA would assume the role of continental policeman in the event that Latin American governments were weakened or incapable. In other words, the United States unilaterally announced both their predominance on the continent and the exclusion of other possible influences in the area.

Latin America intended to contain US expansionism through cooperation and international law. As discussed in Chapter 2, the Argentine politician and intellectual Juan Batista Alberdi was expounding a project for a Latin American Union as early as the mid-1800s, aiming to limit the continental influence of the United States in response to the Monroe Doctrine. The subject of international law went hand in hand with that of Latin American unity. Attempts to limit US power were set in stone at the end of the 1800s with the doctrine of 'sovereign immunity to foreign interference', containing the Calvo clause, which is still applied in many international contracts today. This stipulates that court judgments in one country cannot be subject to appeal abroad if the rights of foreign citizens are involved. Later on, the Drago Doctrine made the further assertion that disputes over foreign debt did not grant creditor countries a right of intervention. Finally, the resolution on non-intervention put forward as a supplement to the Anti-War Pact, which won the Nobel Prize for Argentina's foreign affairs minister Saavedra Llamas in 1936, introduced the principle that no state had the right to intervene in the domestic or foreign affairs of another state. Latin American countries, in a weak position compared to neighbouring powers, thus sought to limit US influence by continental cooperation and the use of international law. All the same, Latin America was and to some degree remains dependent on the

United States both for access to the huge Northern market for the sale of its goods, and as a beneficiary of investments, technological transfers and international aid from Washington.

In the twentieth century, inter-American relations followed the course marked out in the previous century. Periods of strong US unilateralism and interventionism in the rest of the continent alternated with periods of greater respect and cooperation, perhaps dictated more by contingent interests than by any renewed approach from Washington towards Latin America. For example, following the Great Depression triggered by the Wall Street crash in 1929, the United States withdrew into itself to stimulate internal recovery, setting aside its involvement in the rest of the world. Although this resulted in the adoption of a 'good neighbourhood policy' towards Latin American countries, this change was a temporary sideline and was more revealing of a lack of interest in other issues than recognition of the identity and needs of bordering countries.

The Cold War period represented a sort of parenthesis in continental relations. It was a very significant and profoundly influential parenthesis, yet it remained a temporary and somewhat exceptional phase. The main elements of US policy towards Latin America, *in primis* the alternation of more assertive phases with other more cooperative periods depending on the interests and presumed advantages for Washington at different times, did not in fact alter substantially. The three key elements of Washington's foreign policy towards Latin America – advancing US economic interests, guaranteeing its own security, and preventing the influence of extra-continental powers – all remained constant during the Cold War too. What changed were the instruments adopted by Washington to pursue these objectives and the ideological context and contest.

The end of the Second World War introduced a wave of solidarity and complicity on the continent which was enshrined in the 1948 Treaty of Rio for mutual military assistance between the United States and Latin American countries, and in the constitution of the Organization of American States. Moreover, during this time the support of Latin American countries in the newly founded United Nations was vital for building the new international organization according to Washington's desires. The beginning of the Cold War, the USSR's acquisition of the nuclear bomb in 1949, and the fear of communist expansion in Latin America convinced Washington to shift towards a unilateral stance, dictated more by the ideological prism through which the Eisenhower administration viewed the rest of the continent than by objective political or economic considerations. The reformist ambitions of many Latin American countries, still encumbered by the grave problems of underdevelopment and social inequality, were perceived by Washington as having Marxist tendencies, if not hard and fast Soviet infiltrations. As a consequence they were directly or indirectly countered, as demonstrated by the CIA's involvement in overthrowing the democratic and reformist, although not communist, Arbenz government of Guatemala in 1954.

The long-standing burdens of economic and social underdevelopment, however, resulted in the appeal and spread of revolutionary Marxist ideals throughout Latin America. So as the 1950s drew to a close and the 1960s began, the United States opted for a more cooperative relationship with the rest of the continent, with the Alliance for Progress, a political, social and economic development plan for Latin America funded primarily by the USA, as its hub. This plan was based on the assumption that democratic governments would naturally choose to ally with the United States and that this choice would be underpinned by the improvement in living conditions promised by the Alliance for Progress funds. The impossibility of defeating the Cuban revolution led by Fidel Castro, the limited results of the Alliance and the growing demands of Latin American societies, combined with the recrudescence of the Cold War (this was the period of escalation in Vietnam), constrained Washington to abandon this policy of support for democracy and Latin American development in the late 1960s.

The new US position, adopted by the Johnson administration and clarified by the Mann Doctrine, was neutral towards social reforms and political orientations, no longer favouring democratically elected governments but limiting support to regimes capable of meeting US interests and promoting economic growth. This direction was further bolstered under the Nixon administration, which, following the recommendations of the Rockefeller Report, was convinced of growing Marxist infiltration and identified the armed forces of trustworthy Latin American nations as partners in the fight against communism. These were the dark years of dictatorships and human rights abuses in many countries of Latin America during the 1970s.

A new shift occurred when Jimmy Carter became president of the United States in 1976. A staunch advocate of disarmament, nuclear non-proliferation and human rights protection, he tried (albeit in a rather sudden, coarse and unilateral move) to incorporate these convictions into relations between the United States and Latin America, aiming to inject morality into US foreign policy. However, authoritarian Latin American governments, accustomed to Washington's full support and economic aid for fighting communist subversion, were once again wrong-footed by the US government's change of tack. This resulted in rather strained relations on the continent.

When Ronald Reagan became president in 1981 he heralded another political change. Reagan was obsessed by anti-communist hysteria, especially given the heightening of the Cold War following the Soviet invasion of Afghanistan and conflicts in the Horn of Africa and in Angola. The reformist revolution of the Sandinista government in Nicaragua in 1979 convinced him of the need to fight the spread of progressive governments in Central America through legal and illegal means. Reagan supported illegal actions in Nicaragua and El Salvador, and the US administration's conduct was condemned by the UN General Assembly, the International Court of Justice and the US Congress itself. This was during the mid-1980s, when US interest focused on Central America, neglecting the rest of the continent. Perhaps not by chance, these were the years of redemocratization and political renewal in areas of Latin America with less US interference. Argentina, Brazil and Uruguay returned to democracy and sowed the seeds of subregional cooperation projects in South America while Central America was torn by conflict and the small Caribbean island of Grenada was invaded by US marines. At the end of the 1980s, events far from the Latin American continent had a strong impact on international (not only inter-American) relations. The end of the Cold War and the fall of the Soviet empire opened up the door to new paradigms and a world with complex landscapes, problems and equilibriums.

The end of the Cold War and the triumph of the Western camp

de facto marked the termination of the communist threat. The disintegration of the USSR deprived communism of a state paladin which could lead its cause at the international level. Equally the failure of the communist economic and political model left only one winner in the ring: the Western model based on a free market economy and liberal democracy. This model appeared to be the only available solution, and there was almost global consensus that it was the single possible recipe for development and for ensuring harmonious international relations. Optimism and trust abounded for a better world with almost limitless possibilities, providing the setting for the emergence of the neoliberal economic model propagated through the 'Washington Consensus'. This expression was coined by North American economist John Williamson to indicate the convergence of the economic policy preferences of the US government and big international financial institutions such as the World Bank and the International Monetary Fund, both with their headquarters in Washington.[1] These preferences were essentially for trade and market liberalization and a diminished economic role of the state in favour of a widespread privatization process.

In this atmosphere of renewed international cohesion and consensus, the United States inaugurated a policy to promote their winning model in Latin America, favouring the establishment of democratic governments and economic development based on exports and openness to new markets. The pan-American drive which coloured inter-American relations in the 1990s emerged into this context. There was a conviction that all countries, in the North and South, could gain from the deregulation of the economy and international trade. However, in a world without rules, the 'survival of the fittest' precept tends to prevail.

At the beginning of the 1990s President Bush senior proposed the 'Enterprise for the Americas', a project for a single continental economic space stretching from Alaska to Tierra del Fuego. His successor, Bill Clinton, best personified the ambivalence of the US position. On the one hand, he was the primary promoter of summits of the Americas, where heads of state and governments from across the continent would meet to encourage dialogue and cooperation. On the other hand, the USA continued to find new reasons to intervene and interfere in Latin American affairs. The Monroe Doctrine and its corollaries were no longer evoked. In an era of apparent consensus, the promotion of democracy and the fight against drug trafficking and illegal immigration served as justification for the US neo-interventionism in Panama in 1989 and Haiti in 1994. Anachronistic policies such as sanctions and boycotts against Cuba were maintained if not reinforced.

The financial crisis in Mexico in 1994, the Brazilian currency crisis in 1998/99, the political and economic collapse of Argentina in 2001 and the political and institutional legitimacy crisis that pervaded most Latin American countries, besides grave economic difficulties, towards the end of the 1990s revealed the contradictions and limits of the neoliberal model which had inspired Washington's policy towards Latin America during the entire decade. Although some of the neoliberal principles complied with the demands of the industrialized world, they were not necessarily adapted for rapid and generalized application in countries with highly variable levels of development and economies which were as yet unable to rival competition from more developed countries. Despite some successes on a macroeconomic level, the social consequences of the neoliberal era were bound to produce movements rejecting the model.

Since the end of the 1990s and the beginning of the 2000s, Latin America has loudly called for the dismantlement, adaptation or tempering of the neoliberal principles in favour of a policy centred on human and social development. Latin America and its international relations at the dawn of the new millennium were characterized by rebellious sentiments against Washington and the political and economic formulas with which it was associated. A desire for major changes and a renewal of morality affected politics and the economy. The international situation compelled the United States to allow Latin Americans more space and initiative for autonomous and home-grown development, which are becoming the main features of the contemporary landscape.

Inter-American relations in the twenty-first century

The arrival of George W. Bush (junior) at the White House in 2000 aroused an initial degree of expectation in terms of US policy towards Latin America. Bush's campaign and pressing international and regional issues such as migration generated expectations, both in Washington and south of the Rio Bravo, that continental relations would increase at least in status, if not in quality, on the US foreign policy agenda. The events of 9/11 threw into question every item on the previous international agenda of the first Bush junior administration. Latin America became a minor issue. A sufficiently democratic continent, with no weapons of mass destruction, certainly a difficult but not desperate economic situation, and somewhat tenuous links with international terrorism could not be a US priority in the aftermath of 9/11. Experience shows that US neglect of Latin America is not necessarily a bad thing given the poor results in terms of democratic and social development that US interference has often brought about.

A decade into the twenty-first century, regardless of changes of US and Latin American administrations and historical circumstances, there are significant elements of continuity in Washington's policy towards Latin America. The pursuit of stability remains one of the fundamental objectives of Washington's continental policy. At a time when the interests of the international community and its dominant power reside in other areas of the world, the concept of stability in Latin America is clearly intended more as a strategy for avoiding trouble than an active and direct involvement. Even the election of Barack Obama as US president in 2008 has not significantly altered this state of affairs so far, although Washington may become more open towards the rest of the continent following a few policy adjustments in line with Obama's overall foreign policy stance. In fact, within a basic thread of continuity, President Obama's first moves seem to indicate a renewed spirit of cooperation and respect between the North and the South of the Americas. In any case, the USA is more and more likely to concentrate its attention on specific geographic and thematic areas within Latin America.

In the political domain, the main guidelines of Washington's traditional Latin American policy seem to be swinging between obsolescence and new scope for application and redefinition. First, considering that all Latin American countries (with the exception of Cuba) now formally belong to the big democratic family, the task of promoting democracy seems close to completion. As a result of this success and the end of the Cold War, the interests of the Latin American reformist elites and US (even conservative) administrations broadly coincided. However, the new challenge is now the improvement of the quality of democracy – that is to say going beyond its merely formal content of holding reasonably free and fair elections and promoting in turn a more equal and participative society. A US strategy in this respect has still to fully materialize. Secondly, the concept of continental security seems to have undergone a fairly significant revolution. The end of the Cold War was a turning point. Issues such as nuclear proliferation, possible armed conflict or leftist subversion have become obsolete. The fight against drug trafficking, illegal immigration, money laundering and energy and trade security, coupled with the maintenance of democratic rule and a smooth post-Castro transition in Cuba, are cautiously re-examined in Washington as the bulwark of a new US security policy towards the rest of the Americas. Thirdly, the traditional policy of protection of the Western hemisphere from extra-continental interferences might acquire new content and prominence in the light of the booming economic penetration of China in Latin America, together with the increased level of activity of countries such as India, Russia and Iran. Although these developments do not represent a threat in the traditional sense, increased political and economic competition in the Americas may soon present a new type of challenge to US strategic and economic interests. In this context, and with more international options and partners available, including the European Union, Latin American countries now have a much wider range of available solutions to oppose US pre-eminence in the continent. Trade and security issues along with some other more specific aspects deserve particular attention.

Trade relations between the United States and Latin America at the beginning of the new millennium were centred on the plan to build a Free Trade Area of the Americas. Given the difficulties and ensuing stalling of negotiations, the United States, often with the consent of Latin American countries, has favoured switching to a case-by-case approach. One of the main traits of continuity in the US Latin American policy is the attempt to propose, if not impose, its approved rules and economic models on the rest of the continent. The United States, under both Republican and Democratic administrations, has historically been in favour of free markets and deregulation of international trade, but only as long as this is beneficial to the United States. The FTAA would provide ample opportunities to expand US industrial production and services sectors. However, there are still doubts over whether or not Latin American countries also have relevant interests in and potential benefits to gain from the conclusion of such an agreement, or a series of bilateral agreements with the same purpose.

Critics of the FTAA claim that it is simply an instrument for the US to perpetuate its economic hegemony over the Americas in the era of globalization. They claim that it is a tool which uses asymmetric and conditional openness in markets and customs barriers to promote the US economy, providing only negligible benefits for Latin economies. In addition, they state that this openness would result in an intensification of the imbalanced exchange system between the raw materials and agricultural produce of the South and the high-added-value manufactured products of the North, thus exacerbating rather than lessening the disparity in exchange flows. As at the end of the 1800s, Latin American countries, or at least the leading lights among them, hesitate today when faced with a possible pan-American agreement.

Latin America is not a homogeneous entity. Mexico, for obvious geographical reasons, plays a pre-eminent role in Washington's Latin America policy and, as a member of NAFTA, already has guaranteed access to the rich US market. Therefore Mexico has no particular interest in a continent-wide deal that would dilute its advantages and engender more competition from other countries. Moving outwards in concentric circles, the Central American and Caribbean countries come next in order of territorial contiguity and therefore geostrategic relevance to Washington. These countries share the common feature of relatively non-diversified economies which are highly dependent on access to the US market. For Washington, concerns in this area have more to do with security than economic projects, but the latter may have positive implications for the former. The conclusion of free trade agreements, either through the FTAA or bilaterally, is a seemingly crucial requisite for the survival and growth of many of this region's economies. These countries are readily prepared to accept even cumbersome conditions in order to sign these agreements. It is not surprising, then, that, when faced with the difficulties of the FTAA project, a bloc of Central American countries together with the Dominican Republic signed the Dominican Republic–Central America Free Trade Agreement (DR-CAFTA) with the United States. The pink tide, which has also spread to some Central American countries, has not for the moment called this agreement into question, and even the Sandinista president of Nicaragua, Daniel Ortega, has endorsed the deal. This is a clear sign of its importance for signatories of all political persuasions.

It is a different story for the countries of South America, especially those such as Brazil which enjoy significant autonomy, diversified markets and negotiating power. For many of these countries, unlimited access to trade in the US market would certainly be a step forward, albeit one not without conditions and demands. The United States would want to apply restrictions to the free entry of agricultural goods to avoid irritating its own heavily subsidized national producers and their lobbyists. However, agricultural produce is precisely the subject which most interests South American countries as regards the US market. Washington would also want to include dispositions to protect investments in the FTAA negotiations, while Latin American countries would prefer to discuss these in multilateral forums such as the World Trade Organization. Moreover, the countries of South America have more diversified economies, and Europe and increasingly Asia are sufficiently big and rich markets to boost their economies and absorb their exports, especially commodities and crops. The situation is further complicated by ideology. Many progressive-leaning South American countries, especially the most radical ones, have seen opposition to the FTAA negotiations as a way to resist and show hostility to US influence.

Unable to conclude a continental agreement, the United States has pursued the route of free trade agreements with individual countries, thus exerting further pressure on those excluded from this close-knit network of agreements. At the present time, the countries of the Mercosur area are the only ones without any kind of preferential agreement with the United States. The recent conclusion of a framework agreement for investments and trade between the United States and Uruguay has brought the whole Mercosur bloc to the brink of crisis and increased pressure on Uruguayan politicians. If Uruguay decided to accept Washington's offer of a full free trade agreement it would have to renounce virtually all its subregional links, but if it remains faithful to the commitments it has to its neighbours it would have to refuse the advantages that stem from preferential access to the rich US market. This is not simply a commercial deal, the technicalities of which may make it compatible with subregional trade rules. The implications are political, as any such trade agreement has the potential to alter alliances and balances both at the subregional and continental levels.

Security issues shaped inter-American relations during the Cold War. When it ended, the concept of hemispheric security was thoroughly revised. This revision continued in the wake of the 9/11 terrorist attacks.

Traditionally, until the eve of the Second World War, the concept of security for the United States, particularly continental security, had stood for protecting its own interests abroad, free trade, and promoting (preferably democratic) governments amenable to its interests, as well as preventing the rise of regimes that could threaten the peace of the continent or challenge Washington's supremacy. During the Cold War, the conflict between the United States and the Soviet Union stemmed from a series of ideological dichotomies spanning almost every field of social analysis and human activity. There was a philosophical dichotomy between freedom and equality, a political dichotomy between liberal democracy and socialism, and an economic dichotomy between free trade and central planning. Every success, however small, in one of these fields for one of the two camps was considered a victory over the other. Competition in the military field was no exception. Whether through choice or necessity, this meant that other countries had to ally with one of the two camps and pledge not to interact militarily or economically with the other bloc. First and foremost they had to stick to the philosophical, political and economic orthodoxy of the primary power, thus drastically limiting political options and domestic development. For forty-five years inter-American security was based on these criteria. One may well want to ask whose security did this model ensure and what was the exact definition of security adopted. In other words there are now legitimate doubts about whom and what was to be protected at the time. The dignity of man and human development often were not.

When the confrontation of superpowers ended, the ideological polarization also lessened and inter-American relations were repositioned around the traditional dynamics characterizing the period prior to the Cold War. In hemispheric relations, both the United States and Latin American countries have returned to definitions of the 'national interest' centred on domestic well-being, targeting political, economic and social issues rather than ideological and military ones. This turnaround has had considerable effects on security matters. Since the 1990s, for example, the concept of security has come to include matters such as drug trafficking and immigration, which according to the USA have evolved from issues of public order into tangible threats of an international scale.

The invasion of Panama in 1989 was justified by the need to remove General Noriega, accused of international narco-trafficking and electoral fraud. Direct US involvement in anti-narcotics trafficking operations, especially in Colombia but also in Peru and Bolivia, and most recently in Mexico, can be seen from a similar angle. The fight against international narco-trafficking has become a security issue in its own right. The invasion of Haiti in 1994, although it took place after an ambiguous UN resolution, was justified by the urgent need to restore democracy in the country. A more plausible explanation for the Clinton administration's actions was the need to contain flows of Haitian immigrants to the coasts of Florida. The best way to achieve this aim was to stop the massacres perpetrated by the military junta of Haiti. Illegal immigration has thus become a priority again for the inter-American security agenda. This priority is largely imposed by the North on the South. It is unlikely that the United States will revert to direct interventions in Latin America for security reasons, even despite the breadth of this term. There seems not to be any situation that could lead to this becoming a possibility. Latin American terrorism has greatly diminished. In cases where drug trafficking and terrorism are closely related, such as in Colombia, subversive groups seem to be the product of local situations, and links with international terrorist groups, especially Islamic ones, have yet to be proven.

It is plausible that the United States will continue the fight against narcotics trafficking with renewed pragmatism. It is no coincidence, for instance, that Bush junior stopped in Colombia during his 2004 post-electoral trip to Latin America. Until the end of the 1980s, relations between the two countries had traditionally been cordial. The situation deteriorated when the United States made the battle against cocaine a security issue in 1986. The USA's unilateral and disproportionate action ended up provoking the militarization of the domestic Colombian conflict, engendering reactions known as 'narco-terrorism' and 'narco-nationalism'. After a period of difficult relations with both the Samper and Pastrana administrations, the United States has backed President Uribe's effort with ample support and a degree of autonomy, including a $3 billion aid package to combat narcotics production and associated subversion. If the Santos administration, which succeeded Uribe's, were to successfully achieve a solution to terminate the conflict with the FARC and other warring factions, the United States might well be prepared to lower its profile in the international fight against drugs and back local governments from behind the scenes.

Finally, there is the issue of post-Castro transition in Cuba. Here, too, the Cold War had perpetuated, or aggravated, long-standing tendencies. Traditional tensions between the United States and Cuba and the ambitions of the former over the latter were not a product of the post-1959 revolutionary period, but actually have their origins in the mid-nineteenth century. As far back as the 1840s and 1850s there were campaigns in the United States to annex Cuba. Presidents Polk and Pierce tried in vain to acquire it from Spain in the second half of the century. Cuba became independent from Spain only when the US armed forces stepped in. The cost of this was the installation of a de facto protectorate sanctioned by an international treaty in 1903. Even during the 'good neighbourhood' policy years heralded by President Franklin Delano Roosevelt, the United States interfered heavily in political and economic activity on the island.

The Cold War amplified already existing trends. The presence of a Marxist regime just a few miles from the coast of Florida, the missile crisis and Havana's revolutionary activism in Latin America and in Africa transformed Cuba into a security concern. But the end of the bipolar rivalry did not eliminate US animosity towards the Caribbean island. On the contrary, the United States toughened its position in the wake of the Cold War. In 1992, the Torricelli law tightened economic restrictions on international trade with the island. In 1996, the Helms-Burton law further tightened sanctions and unilaterally conferred, without any legal basis for doing so, special prerogatives on the United States in the island's democratization process.

The attitude of the US government remained relatively stable during the two mandates of President George Bush junior. The Bush administration claimed that the normalization of relations with Cuba (in terms of diplomatic recognition, commercial openness and a substantial aid programme) could only occur when Cuba had a fully democratic government. By virtue of the Helms-Burton law, it falls to the US president to decide when the Cuban regime can be described as democratic. In May 2002, Bush also announced an Initiative for a New Cuba, inviting the government of Havana to undertake political and economic reforms and call democratic elections for the Cuban National Assembly. At the same time Bush also declared that the United States posed no threat to the sovereignty of Cuba.

In October 2003, Bush junior also created a Commission for Assistance to a Free Cuba, whose aim was to accelerate a rapid and peaceful transition to democracy. The Commission presented its report to the president in 2004. It suggested the adoption of measures to reinforce civil society in Cuba, break the monopoly on information held by the Castro regime, reduce the flow of resources supporting the regime in Havana, convey a realistic and not idyllic image of Cuban conditions of life and its government abroad, encourage international diplomatic efforts to provoke Castro's departure and weaken the succession strategy outlined by Havana to maintain, as Washington saw it, the same power structures.

When Barack Obama was elected US president, some encouraging signs appeared. Obama acknowledged that Washington's policy towards Cuba had been unsuccessful, thus laying the potential foundations for a substantial reworking of bilateral relations. However, a sudden change of strategy in the next few years is unlikely, especially given the intense pressure exercised by exiled Cuban communities in Florida in favour of the USA's hard line on the Castro regime. For instance, at the April 2009 Summit of the Americas in Trinidad and Tobago, consensus on the final declaration was not achieved because of insurmountable differences between the USA and the other Latin American countries precisely over the Cuban question. It will take time and gradual steps for President Obama to succeed in establishing a different kind of relationship with Cuba to that of his predecessors. Although Cuba is no longer a security problem for the United States, any significant modification to their bilateral relationship will require support and firm political will from both sides.

On the Cuban side, continuity seems to have prevailed on the island with Fidel Castro handing over power to his brother Raúl. In the absence of now unpredictable major domestic upheavals, Cuba will gradually be moving towards economic liberalization, not, however, accompanied by greater political openness. The role model may be China or the other Asian tigers that have based their success on a thriving market economy under tight political control. The outcome remains to be seen. Little is known about the true domestic dynamics within the Castro regime and the position of the military in particular. In the event of a *coup d'état* or a swift natural succession to Raúl (who recently turned seventy), authoritarian revivals or unexpected liberalizations cannot be ruled out. The reaction of the United States will very much depend on domestic events on the island.

The present and future impact of the pink tide on US–Latin American relations

The failure of neoliberalism to deliver sufficient development and prosperity and reduce poverty in Latin America has led to an almost universal reaction on the continent against this development model. Social movements, popular communities, political parties and leaders old and new have fought to oust neoliberal orthodoxy in favour of a stronger focus on society and a marked emphasis on reducing poverty and inequality. This has created a hostile attitude, at least in rhetoric if not in fact, towards neoliberalism and its main exponents, namely the United States. Many of the progressive governments who came to power after 2000 have made it their prerogative to abandon neoliberalism and adopt an international position that is more independent of the United States. But has the current state of inter-American relations truly deteriorated? Has US influence in Latin America really been compromised or just been put on the back burner? The reality is often complex and does not lend itself to simple interpretations.

Analysts and observers disagree over the supposed withdrawal of the US position in Latin America and every evaluation is necessarily dependent on the criteria and parameters adopted. Peter Hakim, director of Inter-American Dialogue, claimed that continental relations were at a historic low in 2006.[2] James Petras, an established international analyst with radical tendencies, spotted a resurgence of US influence in the continent in 2007 compared to just three or four years previously.[3] Larry Birns, director of the Council for Hemispheric Affairs, observed that US ascendancy and influence are no longer automatic but must be deserved and won in some way.[4] In an era of rapid, rather sudden changes of political and economic dependencies and interdependencies, inter-American relations are in a state of fluidity. There does not seem to be a clear linear course or a definitive driving force. It is particularly difficult to identify long-term trends, especially considering that many of the issues linked to continental equilibriums depend on the individual governments in office. Many Latin American countries lack state policies on international relations, contenting themselves instead with government policies which often last only as long as the administration that conceived them. What's certain is that many Latin American countries are redefining their position towards Washington, just as the global (not just continental) role of the United States is being redefined. Once again, there are elements of both continuity and change compared to the past.

The elements of continuity include the long-standing pre-eminent position of the USA as a trade partner for the majority of Latin American countries, the endurance of some approaches to security matters, and a certain ideological affinity between Washington and some Latin American capitals which seems stable despite the proliferation of the pink tide.[5] Even today, the USA absorbs almost 50 per cent of Latin American exports and provides the continent with almost 40 per cent of its imports.[6] The United States could probably survive without Latin America, but perhaps not Mexico. Only 6 per cent of Washington's global trade takes place with the Latin part of the Americas, and US imports of Venezuelan oil represent about 7 per cent of US consumption.[7] In both cases, suppliers and buyers in other geographical areas could replace those in Latin America. But could countries for which Washington represents over half of trade exchanges survive without this partnership? From this perspective, US influence remains practically intact in absolute terms, even if it has perhaps been slightly resized in relative terms. In addition, Washington so far has not been obliged to make any significant concessions to Latin American countries, even in the recently concluded bilateral free trade agreements (FTAs). Subsidies for the US agricultural sector have not slimmed, import quotas on over two hundred important products for Latin American countries have not been removed, and the United States has secured access to the finance, services, high technology, health and education markets in countries that have signed the FTA agreements. Finally, US businesses operating in Latin America have recouped record profits by exploiting the high international prices of raw materials and foodstuffs, which have fed the Latin American economic boom in recent years.

Even the pursuance of security objectives according to traditional definitions does not seem to have suffered significant setbacks because of the arrival of the pink tide. The number of joint military bases and operations between the United States and Latin America has increased during recent years. Washington has bases in Ecuador (although the agreement will not be renewed), El Salvador and Colombia (the deal has recently been expanded). In 2005 a new mega-base was opened in Paraguay, while the progressive Tabaré Vásquez's Uruguay signed agreements for a new military training programme. Joint military exercises take place yearly with almost all Latin American countries except for Cuba and Venezuela. Sales of US weapons and armaments to the majority of progressive Latin American regimes remain almost intact. US anti-narcotics-trafficking and anti-terrorism policies are supported by the overwhelming majority of Latin American countries, even those such as Argentina which have criticized Washington in other areas.

From an ideological point of view too, the rupture between the North and South of the continent is perhaps stronger in rhetoric than in practice. Colombia, Chile and Mexico remain staunch allies of the United States and base their economic fortunes on neoliberal models of development. Moreover, the principles of liberal democracy in politics and the free market in the economy do not seem to have been questioned even by champions of the pink tide except in isolated cases. Lula's and now Dilma's Brazil, whose flagship policy is the fight against poverty, has in fact maintained the neoliberal structure adopted by Collor and deepened by Fernando Henrique Cardoso. Kirchner's Argentina (Nestor first and Cristina later), although it has adopted a heterodox economic strategy, has not renationalized privatized businesses and is continuing with export-based growth. Even supposedly more radical regimes, such as those of Chávez and Morales, have thus far not proceeded with, or successfully implemented, reform programmes which substantially altered the fundamentals of the market economy or the liberal-democratic state. But especially Chávez is now leading Venezuela towards an illiberal democracy and a centrally controlled and constrained market economy.

All this raises the question: to what extent is the pink tide a threat or challenge to Washington? It should be understood that 'threat' here is not intended in the military sense. However, what's certain is that the pink tide, especially its most forthcoming components, has the potential to change dependency relationships between the two halves of the continent. The reason for this is not only the new development- and autonomy-based ideological approach, but also the conditions of the international landscape during the globalization era. Although often accused of favouring the wealthy and well off to the detriment of the weak, globalization also provides an immense impetus for democratization, a diffusion of power and knowledge which tends to erode the capacity of all economic and political structures to control and dominate, and makes all kinds of relationships interdependent with many others, thus favouring processes of accommodation and negotiation to help the international system run. Given this situation, both the increased autonomy from Washington in some Latin American countries and the meanings of the words 'threat' and 'challenge' are closely bound to interconnections with globalization.

In terms of major negotiating power and autonomy in foreign policy, some Latin American governments are certainly making use of the renewed ideological and nationalist pull associated with the pink tide, but international factors remain paramount. The high prices of minerals and foodstuffs on world markets have allowed many countries in the area to temporarily overcome their payment imbalance problems. As a consequence these countries no longer need urgent loans from the International Monetary Fund and are thus less subject to economic policy ties and structural adjustments often imposed by the IMF with the agreement of the United States. The enhanced availability of liquidity also gives these countries more room for manoeuvre in their development projects, reducing the need to turn to funds from the World Bank and accept its conditions, which are often shaped by Washington. What's more, the rise of China and other Asian economic powers provides an alternative to US markets, investments and loans, further diminishing the gap in negotiating power between the North and South of the continent. These international events in fact stimulate autonomy and diversification in foreign policy choices for many Latin American countries.

A similar reasoning applies to the supposed or perceived challenges which the pink tide and more broadly twenty-first-century Latin America may pose to Washington. It is not difficult to see that the achievement of the US objectives in Latin America – political and economic stability, immigration, the fight against drugs trafficking and terrorism and the expansion of trade opportunities – depends more on international factors rather than the internal choices of any single country. Proactive cooperation between several states is required to control migratory flows and the fight against drugs trafficking and terrorism. This has the potential to increase Latin

American negotiating power vis-à-vis Washington, but cooperation is also and perhaps foremost in US interests because failures in these areas could increase the danger and threat for Washington. A poor and underdeveloped Latin America could potentially create mass illegal immigration flows to the United States. Ongoing violence in many Latin American cities could result in a northward expansion of gang wars and trafficking of arms, drugs and human beings. An inefficient health system could result in an outbreak of new epidemics which could easily cross geographical and political borders. Thus it is in the interests of the United States to work towards harmonious economic and social development on the Latin American continent, focusing on opportunities and not just challenges. In fact, from a US perspective, Latin America is an as yet practically untapped potential market: Argentina, Colombia and Venezuela alone, for instance, constitute a market of 100 million consumers. The problem at the moment is that significant parts of their population live in poverty and/or cannot afford high levels of consumption. Whether or not it is desirable to reduce any and every issue to a matter of consumption levels and potential markets is a different question altogether.

What could the United States do to encourage better relations with the rest of the continent? There is undoubtedly a degree of disappointment on both sides. Proposals have come from various directions suggesting that the United States should adopt a similar approach regarding Latin America to that of the European Union with its neighbours or indeed accession candidates. Essentially, this would mean transferring resources from richer to poorer areas. Assuming the United States has no moral or legal obligations to embark on such projects, it is unclear whether such involvement would be well received. Latin America often tends to complain about Washington's lack of commitment towards the rest of the continent, only to suffer the negative consequences when this commitment occurs. A kind of Marshall Plan for the Americas does not yet seem plausible. First, the cooperation method preferred by Washington is 'trade not aid'. Secondly, and most importantly, the USA lacks the political will and economic resources to embark on such a venture. The cumbersome expenses of the war in Iraq, reconstruction post-hurricane Katrina, and the pressure on federal finances due to the tax cuts imposed by the Bush junior administration and the anti-crisis rescue plan and stimulus package of the Obama administration make major US projects in Latin America unlikely.

However, simply basing hemispheric relations on trade and political alliances in international forums is not enough to relaunch pan-Americanism or deal with poverty and inequality. A comparison with the European Union, however unsuitable it may seem, helps to define the problem. A few years after joining the European Union, the GDPs of Spain and Portugal were aligned with the European average. After fifteen years in NAFTA, Mexico's GDP, although it grew in absolute terms, lost ground compared to that of the United States in relative terms, and Mexican GNI per capita is less than one fifth of the USA's.[8] Miguel Angel Centeno of the University of Princeton presents as one possible solution the creation of a new hemispheric model for cooperation in which the United States and Canada would offer access to their own markets, including the labour market, to Latin American countries that reach the same standards as those of North America in the health, employment and environment sectors.[9] This proposal, however, seems lacking in pragmatism. Where would Latin American countries, especially the poorest ones, find the resources to reach the standards required by Washington? What's more, the United States has no need to set these targets: improving health, employment and environment conditions is already a priority for many Latin American governments. Countries that possess the economic resources to sustain such development programmes (e.g. Mexico, Brazil and Chile) are already approaching the targets or have made huge advances. Those which lack such resources cannot activate the necessary development policies. This seems to be a vicious circle. Unrestricted access to the North American market would allow those countries to collect resources for development. Making development a criterion for access to the North American market does not really seem to solve the basic problem: poverty generates poverty whereas wealth generates wealth.

The reality is that Latin America itself must find the moral resources and political and economic solutions to fund its own development. Relations with the United States could be as much a hindrance as a resource in this matter. Without doubt, evaluating continental relations using the 1990s and the neoliberal paradigm as points of reference is to say the least a false exercise. The 1990s was an era of incredible and probably unique ideological, political and economic convergence within the American continent and elsewhere. It is therefore unfair to evaluate pre- and post-1990s inter-American relations with reference to that situation.[10] The phenomenon of the pink tide and its impact on pan-American relations has to be interpreted not primarily as an outright rejection of globalization with anti-American accents but rather as a very legitimate quest for a more equal and equitable political and economic order, continentally and globally. The request for a free trade area based on fairer criteria with dividends for all participants should not be confused with anti-imperialist rhetoric. In the new global panorama, North America and Latin America need to get along and come to terms with each other's requirements. The United States will have to be willing to accommodate and make concessions to Latin American conditions. The USA may also consider that in the absence of such attention, extra-continental powers, established and emerging, may gain significant space in Latin America.

Relations with the European Union

Relations between Europe and Latin America have a long and deep-seated history. Latin America was colonized primarily by Spain and Portugal, and events that took place in Europe, such as the Napoleonic wars, were at the root of Latin American independence in the early nineteenth century. Up until the end of the First World War the wealth of many Latin American countries, for example Argentina, was dependent upon commercial ties with European powers, particularly Great Britain. Following the Second World War and with the onset of the Cold War, European former colonial powers lost their status as world powers and relations with Latin America were put on the back burner. The establishment of the European Economic Community in 1957 did little to reverse this trend, and Latin America increasingly became a sideline in European international affairs. However, when Spain and Portugal joined the European Union in 1986, relations between the EU and Latin America took on a new elan, with European political and economic presence reaching new heights. Latin America has not become a priority area for the EU; quite the contrary in fact. Nonetheless, in its strategy as a global player the EU has adopted a rather active and dynamic position regarding Latin America.

Nowadays, the European Union is an essential partner for Latin America. It is the first provider of development cooperation in the area, the second trade partner (but the first for Mercosur and Chile) after the United States, and a leading investor competing with the USA for the first rank. According to European Union statistics,[11] trade exchanges with Latin America more than doubled between 1990 and 2005. European imports reached €67 billion in 2005, while in the same year exports amounted to €58 billion, providing Latin America with a trade surplus of almost €10 billion. This trend is being consolidated as Latin American exports to the EU in recent years have grown at a markedly higher rate than imports. In particular, Europe imports mining products, fuels, foodstuffs and transport parts. Most of its exports are concentrated in the sectors of industrial and financial products, mainly machinery, chemicals and transport equipment. For the Mercosur countries, the EU is both the main trade partner and the primary supplier of direct foreign investment. European businesses, especially in Spain, played a key role in privatizations during the 1990s, particularly in the banking, telecoms, energy and aviation sectors.

The EU has made South America a privileged recipient of investments. In 2009 Brazil alone absorbed about 40 per cent of European direct foreign investment, while Argentina has replaced Mexico as the second-largest recipient.[12] However, during the past few years the role of the EU as an investor in Latin America has somewhat waned. This is due to a variety of factors, including a decline in Spanish investments (Spain and the Netherlands being the main European investors in the area, followed by France, the United Kingdom and Germany), the growth of China and other Asian powers, the stable position of the United States and the absence of better opportunities formerly provided by privatizations.

An essential aspect when evaluating the importance of the European Union for Latin America is the fact that it also represents a desirable and sustainable model for development. European integration is often used as an example by the Latin American ruling elite when building their own models for integration and establishing their aims, and pursuing models, of sustainable development and a social state, often in opposition to the US example. The EU also offers a possible alternative to US influence as a political and trade partner and an ally in multilateral forums. Finally, Europe is the region of the world whose history, culture and identity are most closely intertwined with those of Latin American countries. Many of them, particularly the most socially advanced countries such as Argentina, Uruguay and Chile, claim a quasi-European status in order to stand out from the rest of the continent.

The EU sustains a complex network of relationships with Latin America in politics, the economic/trade sector and in cooperation for development. This mesh shapes the relational and development model which Brussels offers to Latin America: a complete and structured platform with substantial differences to that of the United States, deeply rooted in the commercial sector and in which political dialogue is almost exclusively bilateral and through the Organization of American States. Furthermore, the model of relations proposed by the EU interacts with Latin America at several levels with specific mechanisms and institutions: regional, subregional, bilateral and through civil society exchanges fuelled by EU dedicated programmes. Although a degree of continuity can be identified in Brussels' preference for and support of region-to-region relations – or inter-regionalism, that is between the EU as a whole and regional or subregional groups in Latin America – there are also some signs of change, especially in the case of Brazil, now recognized by the EU as a special partner which cannot be ignored and can stand alone in Latin American affairs.

The thematic and geographical variety of the EU relational model with Latin America certainly has immense advantages, but is not without its drawbacks. It is somewhat dispersive, rarely leads to significant decisions and commitments, and is very expensive to keep ticking over. Europe's approach to Latin America is a perfect embodiment of the soft power for which the EU is known worldwide, namely with a global presence and power based more on dialogue, values, positive incentives and commercial influence than military force and imposition.

On the bi-regional level, there are two official mechanisms for political dialogue between Europe and Latin America: EU–Latin America/Caribbean summits and EU–Rio Group summits. The first are biennial bilateral meetings between heads of state and government which identify the basic drivers and priorities for the bi-regional relationship. The first summit took place in Rio de Janeiro in 1999 and the latest in Madrid in 2010. This one may well have marked the end of an era and a cooperation model. The EU is not any more in a position to dictate the agenda because it underwrites most of the expenses related to the summits. The next meeting, in Santiago de Chile in 2012, will hopefully inaugurate a new, more truly bilateral phase in which both cost and benefits will be equally shared. The Rio Group was created during the mid-1980s by a small group of Latin American countries to support democratic consolidation. It later expanded to include almost all of the countries on the continent, and even Cuba joined in 2008. The EU–Rio Group summits of ministers take place every two years, alternating with the EU–Latin America summits. The last two of these summits, held in Santo Domingo in 2007 and Prague in 2009, have significantly marked the EU–Latin American agenda. During the former, pressing international concerns such as the rising importance of energy, the environment and climate change were discussed, and the intention of closer collaboration in multilateral forums was reaffirmed, especially in the areas of human rights, drug trafficking and the prevention and management of crises and international conflicts. In Prague, two key issues were discussed: renewable sources of energy and recovery of financial stability and the growth of the world economy after the global crisis. Interestingly, while Latin America has suffered limited damage from the crisis and has promptly recovered, the EU is still struggling, especially with the problems of Greece, Portugal, Ireland, Spain and Italy.

Discussions at the Santo Domingo EU–Rio Group summit led to the definition of the European Commission's new 2007–2013 Strategy for Latin America, which defined the specific areas for regional development cooperation programmes. The regional strategy document adopted by the Commission outlines a yearly EU pledge of over €500 million and identifies five priority action areas: social cohesion including combating poverty and inequality, support for Latin American regional integration, greater transparency and good governance, the establishment of a common EU–Latin American area for higher education, and sustainable development.[13] Overall, the EU general policy priorities towards Latin America remain those defined in the Commission Communication *EU–Latin America: Global Players in Partnership* of 2009.[14]

Another key feature of EU relations with Latin America is the so-called 'horizontal cooperation programmes' that the EU has successfully carried out over the years to support Latin American development and relations between the two continents in a variety of thematic areas. Some of the most valid programmes were Al-Invest, which supported European SMEs interested in investing in Latin America, Alfa and Alban for cooperation in the higher education sector, Urbal for the creation of direct links between cities, @LIS to promote the information society and reduce the digital technology gap in Latin America, and Eurosocial, aimed at reinforcing social cohesion and reducing inequality through action in the health, education, employment and justice sectors and the reform of public administration. These programmes are broadly part of the Union 'region to region' approach, considering Latin America and the Caribbean as a macro-region of reference, but the EU also acts on a subregional level. Formal and institutionalized mechanisms of interaction exist with Mercosur, the Andean Community and Central America. All these subregional relations are articulated in three interconnected strategic fields: political dialogue, development cooperation, and trade and investments.

The Mercosur area has the strongest and deepest historical and cultural bonds with Europe. It is thus unsurprising that this area also has the strongest political and economic ties with the EU. The EU has always assisted Mercosur as part of its support strategy for regional integration schemes elsewhere in the world, and by 1992, just one year after the Treaty of Asunción, the EU had made an agreement to supply the newly formed South American bloc with technical assistance. Although a possible EU–Mercosur association agreement is in the pipeline (see below), relations between the two blocs at the moment are amply regulated by the 1995 Framework Agreement for Inter-regional Cooperation, which covers three fields: political dialogue, cooperation and commercial issues.

Political dialogue took shape in 1996 and includes meetings between heads of state and government, ministers and diplomats. These meetings usually take place in tandem with the EU–Latin American and Caribbean summits to save time and economic resources. The key themes on the current agenda are the conclusion of the EU–Mercosur association agreement, better coordination of positions in multilateral forums, and intensification of cooperation in innovation and technology. Subregional cooperation, which is a complement to EU cooperation with individual member states in Mercosur, concentrates on assistance to help complete the common market of Mercosur and reinforce regional institutions and civil society. In particular, Union funds were used to support the Mercosur secretariat and the conflict resolution instrument, as well as measures for harmonization in the customs, statistical, veterinary and macroeconomic sectors. The EU is Mercosur's main trade partner: it accounts for over 20 per cent of the bloc's commercial relations and is the primary supplier of direct investments, which, it must be said, amount to only 3.5 per cent of the EU's total foreign direct investments.[15]

Given their political and economic links, it seems logical for the EU and Mercosur to strengthen their exchanges by concluding an association agreement on the commercial liberalization of goods and services and creating a free trade area. Initially at least, the European Union's interests lay in the growing export flow towards Mercosur during the second half of the 1990s before this trend was reversed in recent years. In areas which are of significant interest to the EU, such as the automotive sector, the restrictions enforced by Mercosur were a major issue. The incentives for Mercosur were the comparative advantages enjoyed by its agricultural and food products and the hope of reducing the commercial deficit of the 1990s (by now reversed into surplus). There were also defensive factors: the EU feared losing market quotas in the area following the conclusion of the (later suspended) Free Trade Area of the Americas, while the Mercosur countries were apprehensive about the EU's eastward enlargement, fearing that EU resources would be directed elsewhere. Later, some of these motivations subsided and the association talks which had begun in 1999 ground to a halt in 2004. The EU decided to relaunch the negotiations in 2010.

There were multiple and complex reasons for this lack of progress between 2004 and 2010. As well as the changing international situation, particularly the shifting trends and equilibriums in trade surpluses which have altered the interests and strategies at play, it is important to note that the bilateral association agreement was closely linked with multilateral negotiations on similar topics within the World Trade Organization. The multilateral draft under discussion at the WTO was more favourable to Mercosur countries than the EU bilateral proposal. For this reason, the parties prioritized multilateral discussions, at least until summer 2006, when the collapse of the Doha Round provided a possible incentive to re-engage in bilateral dialogue. However, other difficulties existed. The European Commission's own estimates confirm that a potential liberalization, whether partial or complete, would have relatively more positive effects for the EU than for Mercosur. This can be explained by the fact that over 60 per cent of products that Mercosur countries export to the Union are already free from import duty. This is true for both industrial and agricultural products.[16] On the other hand, the EU's most important export sectors (automotive, transport components, mechanical and electrical products) are subject to relatively high customs duties when entering Mercosur. Considering that the European Union also has an undeniable comparative advantage in services and investments, the inclusion of these sectors in the free trade agreement linked to the association agreement would be another advantage for Europe. More importantly, the EU does not seem inclined to make significant concessions in the agricultural domain, which remains the key interest for Mercosur countries.

The relaunch of negotiations in 2010 is due to a number of factors which may now provide enough incentive for a successful conclusion of the association agreement. First, the rise of China forces the EU to look for new markets to compete globally and to defend more effectively its market quota abroad. China also offers Mercosur countries an alternative trade partner to the USA and the EU, thus increasing their leverage with the latter. Secondly, the stalemate of multilateral negotiations at the WTO seems endless, which increases the convenience of the bilateral option to both parties. Thirdly, the global crisis that shook the EU hard requires strategies to reactivate growth and employment, and fostering trade relations with Mercosur may be part of such a strategy. Fourthly, Brazil's rise ought to produce tangible results in terms of commercial expansion. The Lula administration was unable to produce any significant trade preferential agreement but it is in the area of trade that big powers and would-be ones will increasingly compete globally. Brazil needs some success in this domain, and the association agreement with the EU may serve this purpose as well as reinforce Brazil's credentials as leader of Mercosur and South America.

The type of relation which the EU has built with the Andean Community and Central America follows the same structure as that with Mercosur, namely political dialogue, trade and investment, and development cooperation. More recently, a modification of format and substantial progress on trade agreements have been made. Political dialogue with the Andean Community, initiated during the mid-1990s, takes place between presidents and ministers and usually coincides with other major events such as Rio Group meetings. Traditionally, the main areas of interest have been support for democratic institutions, respect for human rights and the consolidation of integration procedures. A new agreement was formed in 2003 extending political dialogue to topics such as conflict prevention, good governance, emigration and terrorism. However, the topic that typifies EU–Andean Community relations remains the fight against drug trafficking, and the principle of shared responsibility between parties in this battle has been established. The EU is the primary donor to Andean countries in terms of cooperation for development, Bolivia being the main recipient.

Commercial relations between the EU and the Andean Community remain modest and often one-directional. The Andean area represents less than 1 per cent of the EU commercial flows, mainly composed of manufactured industrial products, while the EU represents 15 per cent of Andean commercial traffic, mainly agricultural produce.[17] We must also bear in mind that many Andean countries, especially the poorest, enjoy privileged conditions for access to the EU market, although this access is sometimes conditional upon the completion of political and institutional reforms. Negotiations for an EU–Andean Community association agreement, including political dialogue, trade and development cooperation, were launched in 2007 but collapsed in 2008. The EU then modified its traditional strategy, offering the continuation of the EU–Andean Community (as a whole) political dialogue and development cooperation chapters, while splitting trade negotiations geographically. In 2010 negotiations were successfully concluded with Peru and Colombia while Ecuador withdrew from the process in 2009 and Bolivia decided not to participate in the venture following Evo Morales' anti-free-trade position.

EU–Central America relations are also articulated on the three pillars of political dialogue, trade and development cooperation. Political dialogue between the European Union and Central America is deeply entrenched in history. During the mid-1980s, against a backdrop of war and insurrection in the countries of the isthmus, the then European Economic Community launched the 'San José dialogue' to seek solutions to the Central American conflict, enhancing these efforts with an economic aid package to tackle the roots of the problem. In 1993, Central American countries adopted a new institutional framework for regional integration, the Sistema de Integración Centroamericana (SICA), including a Central American Court of Justice, a regional parliament and a secretariat general. Since then significant progress has been made towards economic integration in Central America. At the 2006 EU–Latin America summit held in Vienna, the two parties decided to open negotiations on an association agreement, including a free trade area. In May 2010 negotiations were successfully concluded and representatives of the two parties initialled the text of a comprehensive Association Agreement in March 2011. European cooperation for development in Central America has always been, at least in relative terms, fairly robust, giving priority to areas such as human rights, rural development, prevention of natural disasters (including reconstruction programmes such as the €250 million paid out after Hurricane Mitch), social development and vital support for regional integration. In the trade and investment sectors, the EU is Central America's second-biggest partner. The EU accounts for 12 per cent of Central America's trade exchanges,[18] after the United States, which easily takes first place with 46 per cent. As is the case for the Andean Community, the fight against drug trafficking is a crucial element of Brussels' relations with Central America too. The Commission has adopted a system of customs preferences to reward those countries most active in fighting narcotics production and trafficking.

There are currently three exceptions to the EU's preference for inter-regional relations. The first two, Chile and Mexico, for questions of *force majeure*, since neither is a full participant in genuinely Latin American integration schemes. The third, Brazil, is a matter of choice owing to its preponderant political and economic weight in the continent. This choice in fact could represent a mid-term strategic adjustment in Brussels' view of international relations towards Latin America and beyond, recognizing the necessity of complementing region-to-region approaches with direct bilateral links with powerful regional or subregional leading countries where appropriate. Chile is not a full member of any regional integration scheme: it is an associate member of both Mercosur and the Andean Community. This has necessarily compelled the EU to adopt an ad hoc relations programme. Moreover, Chile enjoys middle to high levels of per capita income and a stable, healthy and diversified economy, with appreciably high levels of competitiveness and low levels of corruption. In order to strengthen bilateral relations after Chile's return to democracy, the EU concluded its first cooperation framework agreement in 1990 and signed an association agreement covering political dialogue, cooperation and trade relations (including a free trade area) in 2002. According to EU data, trade flows between the EU and Chile have practically doubled since the association agreement came into force in 2005. This explains why other Latin American countries are extremely interested in such options. Given Chile's advanced level of development, cooperation has been more sophisticated than in other areas in Latin America and focuses at present on social cohesion, higher education, innovation and competitiveness.

Mexico is the only Latin American country which belongs to a regional integration scheme with industrialized countries (NAFTA) and is a member of the Organisation for Economic Co-operation and Development (OECD). Based on these considerations, the EU decided to entertain with Mexico an ad hoc programme of relations. EU–Mexico relations are regulated by the 1997 Economic Partnership, Political Coordination and Cooperation Agreement, which entered into force in 2000. A free trade area for goods and services was also agreed. Political dialogue is ample and well developed and covers all bilateral and international topics of mutual interest and all levels of meetings, i.e. between presidents, ministers and diplomats. In the first six years following the entry into force of the free trade agreement, commercial flows almost doubled and European direct foreign investment in Mexico shot up by 120 per cent. EU cooperation with Mexico is concentrated in areas such as the protection of tropical forests, expansion of the tertiary sector, demographic policies, justice and human rights, and science and technology. Priorities for the 2007–13 period include social cohesion, competitiveness, education and culture.

The third case of ad hoc relationship, Brazil, is certainly the most interesting from a political perspective. Up until 2007, EU–Brazil dialogue essentially took place via EU–Mercosur summits. At that point, bilateral relations accelerated decidedly, culminating in the first EU–Brazil summit in Lisbon in July 2007. On that occasion, Benita Ferrero-Waldner, the then EU Commissioner for External Relations, clearly explained the reasons for this shift in European policy: Brazil is a pillar of stability in South America and has emerged as a champion of developing countries within the United Nations. The Commissioner also made explicit the objectives of this 'special relationship': the EU commits itself strongly to a strategic partnership with Brazil and to develop it at the multilateral, regional and bilateral level with the conviction that this can lead to the conclusion of the association agreement with Mercosur. Brazil is preparing to become a world power, and the ability to rely on its support in various international arenas is an important variable for EU foreign policy. Brazil is already the biggest EU market in Latin America (around a third of traffic), and the Union accounts for around 20 per cent of Brazil's total commercial flows. Priorities for the 2007–13 period focus on the improvement of bilateral relations through sectoral dialogues, especially in the fields of education, protection of the environment and sustainable development.

Relations with China: return to Eldorado or return to dependency?

Commercial exchanges and political relations between China and Latin America have witnessed an exponential explosion. According to data from the UN Economic Commission for Latin America and the Caribbean (ECLAC), Chinese exports to Latin America and the Caribbean grew by 17.8 per cent between 1995 and 2000, by 26.8 per cent between 2000 and 2005, and by 26.1 per cent between 2005 and 2009. Chinese imports over the same periods of time have increased by 12.7 per cent, 37.6 per cent and 22.8 per cent respectively. Currently, Latin America and the Caribbean account for about 6 per cent of Chinese total trading flows both for import and export. In 2009 Latin American exports to China accounted for about 7 per cent of the total export of the region, against the 40 per cent share of the United States and the 14 per cent of the European Union.[19] This means that the absolute values are still relatively low. Nonetheless, these tendencies are very significant. If they remain constant, ECLAC estimates suggest that China may overhaul the EU as the region's second trade partner by 2015.

During his 2004 Latin American tour, President Hu Jintao promised massive Chinese investment to support Latin American development of transport and communication infrastructure. He also promised further growth in trade and granted Argentina and Brazil the status of 'approved' tourist destinations. Obviously China expects something in return from its presence in Latin America. The 2004 tour secured Argentina, Brazil and Chile's recognition of China as a country with a market economy status. The main practical consequence is that it will be more difficult to begin anti-dumping procedures against growing exports of low-cost Chinese manufactured goods on international markets. The rapid growth in industry and the gross domestic product and the relative scarcity of agricultural land make China an insatiable consumer of primary agricultural produce and natural resources, which South American countries have in large quantities and are anxious to export. Also, an improved transport and communication network in Latin America would represent a doubly profitable investment for Beijing, which could be supplied by those markets in greater quantities, in shorter times and at lower prices, with a good return for both parties.

In the light of this situation, China's presence has raised hopes of economic growth and new job creation in Latin America. Indeed, most of the continent's growth in the last few years is largely related to exports to China and the Asian markets which helped Latin America surf through the global crisis. China also has the not inconsiderable advantage of being a possible alternative to the United States and the often US-dominated international institutions as a provider of capital and technology. However, excessive optimism might be dangerous. The relevance of China as a trading partner hides several challenges. China exports to Latin America much more than it imports, which has generated a growing trade deficit. China tends to import natural resources and foodstuffs while exporting manufactured products, a pattern that in the past has hampered development and created situations of dependency. China's interest in Latin America is limited to a few countries, namely Brazil, Chile, Argentina, Mexico and Peru (and to a lesser extent Venezuela and Costa Rica) and a few products, namely soy, copper, iron ore, zinc, nickel and sugar. Isn't this reminiscent of old colonial or imperial patterns? The environmental costs associated with the expansion of farmland and mining activities could also be very high for Latin America. The true impact and duration of China's effect on the economy and political choices of Latin America must be assessed with caution.

The Chinese model of penetration should make Latin Americans wary of new dependencies which bear resemblances to old or new forms of colonialism. For example, support for better infrastructures harks back to a basic concept of European, especially English, colonialism, as getting supplies from far-off lands can be difficult and lack competitiveness if methods of transport are inadequate. It is in China's interest to develop infrastructure in Latin America, but only such infrastructure as is useful to link extraction or harvest sites to port and other shipping facilities servicing routes to Asia. Moreover, investments that target the mining and extraction sectors can easily degenerate into exploitation, as aptly demonstrated by North American extraction companies in Latin America. And in the past benefits from the mining industry, such as expectations of job creation and economic and social improvement for local communities, have remained quite limited. Finally, and this is perhaps the greatest risk, the nature of Chinese investments is not yet obvious. If these were to materialize in the form of tied loans (low-interest loans for projects commissioned to Chinese businesses) as they may well do, this would result in a real risk of new debt in the form of payments for the allocated orders.

In the long term, then, what may at first appear a 'jackpot' for Latin America could turn out to be a red herring. By improving their current economic situation through selling to China, South American countries contribute to the Asian country's rapid growth and swift penetration of the global manufactured goods markets. In time, China could end up replacing some of those same Latin American added-value export products. Andean and Central American countries already fear that with the deregulation of the textile industry, Chinese products could become impossible to rival not only on the US market but on their own domestic markets. Brazilian automobile producers already see the Chinese as formidable competitors in the Latin American market for medium- to low-cost car parts. The cost of labour in Latin America rules out competition with China on low-cost goods, and the fact that China is rapidly shrinking the technological gap with more advanced economies implies that the Asian giant could soon replace North American and European competitors in Latin American countries.

The step from economic dependency to a loss of political autonomy is not very big. The model already in place with the United States would be reproduced. Countries highly dependent on the US or Chinese markets would be prepared to pay the price of sizeable political concessions, for example in international forums, in order not to lose or to increase access of their own exports to destination markets. For the United States, Chinese competition is one of the major challenges on the world markets for the next few years.

Allowing one of its main competitors a dominant position over such a close neighbour, Latin America, is not an attractive prospect for Washington. The Monroe Doctrine is not expected to be revived, at least not openly, to curb the potentially swelling influence of China or indeed other emerging Asian economies. However, to avoid losing ground in Latin America the United States could begin to revise and adjust its continental strategy. It is not by chance that the three most hotly tipped candidates for the US presidential seat in 2008, John McCain, Barack Obama and Hillary Clinton, all stressed the need for the USA to renew its approach to the rest of the continent. Nonetheless, so far the new president has more or less maintained continuity with the previous US policy on Latin America, and his 2011 trip to Brazil, Chile and El Salvador has not introduced any significant element of novelty.

The evolution of relations between China and Latin America (or rather South America) could depend to a great extent on relations between Brazil and China and the international positions of these powers. If Brazil assumes a leading role in South America, taking on its burdens and associated costs too, it could negotiate more favourable conditions for relations with China on behalf of the whole continent. Perhaps in such a case China would not dare to challenge the regional leader on its doorstep. In other words, this is a similar game to the one Brazil and Latin America may be able to play with the United States. Because of its economic characteristics and strengths, Brazil has room for manoeuvre even with Washington that others countries cannot afford. If Brazil were to succeed in becoming a world player during the next few years, its many common interests with the international agenda of the United States (biofuels, agricultural and industrial markets and energy supply) and China (the development agenda, trade, environment and energy) could benefit the whole region as Brazil champions its interests internationally. In any case, it may still be premature to evaluate China's influence in Latin America. Judging by the percentages, exchanges between China and Latin America are expanding a great deal, but we must remember that the starting point was low. Thus, in real terms, the upsurge has been less spectacular although very significant. It remains to be seen for how long China's presence in

Latin America will continue to grow at the same speed and which international strategies Beijing leaders will decide to follow in the medium and long term.

Conclusions

Latin America's international relations in the twenty-first century reveal traits of continuity and elements of change from the past. The United States continues to be an inescapable factor influencing Latin America's international position. Because of its geographical proximity, Latin America is both a political and a commercial partner for Washington as well as a strategic area for security issues, albeit in a quite broad sense of the term, including, for example, the fight against narcotics trafficking and illegal immigration. However, Latin America seems today to have a much wider variety of options on the international scene than in the past, as well as more room for manoeuvre in relation to its northern neighbour. This is due less to the impact of the pink tide than to the changing international situation, such as the end of the Cold War and of the neoliberal consensus, high prices of export products and, in particular, the growing presence and availability of economic and political partners such as the European Union, China and other new emerging powers. Renewed efforts for South–South cooperation (the IBSA initiative: India, Brazil and South Africa), agreements between emerging powers (the BRIC group: Brazil, Russia, India and China) and new alliances in multilateral forums (the G20 and the Cairns Group in the WTO, the new G20 for financial affairs) seem to be increasing Latin America's presence and influence in the global arena, especially with Brazil's potential role of great power.

With greater autonomy and assertiveness in foreign relations, Latin America finally seems to be displaying a considerable degree of pragmatism in its international projection and strategies. The use of hyperbolic rhetoric is often deployed to emphasize national and regional interests and is seldom accompanied by inflexible and insurmountable ideological postures. Brazil seems ready to exercise regional leadership, thus increasing its own influence and that of the continent on the global scene. But is the continent ready to accept it? For the time being attempts at integration and aggregation are numerous, but perhaps what is really missing is truly regional unity. Piling up is not the same as integrating. If the current phase of international success and recognition is to be consolidated and improved, the quality of governance in the continent and a common vision for the future are indispensable. Otherwise, either this upward phase will be merely contingent or it will benefit only a few among and within Latin American countries.

Conclusion

After the first decade of the twenty-first century, Latin America faces enormous challenges but also has great opportunities. Most of all, it has made huge progress in all departments, from economic growth and stability to democratic consolidation, social development and influence in world affairs. In spite of the many remaining problems and the difficult tasks ahead, it is fair to say that Latin America is now probably in a better situation than ever before. All Latin American countries except Cuba are democracies, many of them strong and consolidated. Latin America has never experienced such a dramatic decrease in its poverty and inequality levels. Even the poor, the marginalized and the indigenous populations now enjoy political representation, and social matters are at the heart of domestic and international agendas. Poverty is falling throughout the continent, at steady rates in some areas, and perhaps for the first time social inequalities seem to be shrinking rather than growing. With Latin American exports selling at high prices on international markets, the economy is growing steadily across the continent. This trend continued even during the global economic crisis that started in 2008, and economic forecasts are quite positive.

There is thus reason for cautious optimism over the future of Latin America. However, there are still serious problems and significant challenges. There are still large pockets of poverty and social inequality; violence, crime and insecurity in some countries, or areas of them, remain high; democracy in some countries may degenerate into illiberal regimes, albeit formally elected, and there are differing degrees of inclination towards the populism that caused more problems than it solved in the past. Economic and technological dependency on industrialized countries seems to have dwindled, but may simply have changed in appearance: the stability of export markets and the level of international prices are two variables which are prone to change and cycles.

At the state level, Latin America is experiencing a wave of progressive governments which emphasize social issues and the fight against poverty. This movement is neither simple nor uniform, but composite and varied. There are differences in economic management, the vision of the state and democracy, and international relations. The social commitment, the economic and social role of the state and a highly personalized politics are the most obvious common features. Although many of these administrations have broken with the neoliberal period of the 1990s, many continue to adhere to neoliberal economic precepts, while only a minority has rejected them completely. The neoliberal era, it is helpful to recall, has by no means been a total catastrophe. The social price of the neoliberal reforms was certainly too high and a more gradual and considerate approach would have been desirable. It is also true that the neoliberal experience has left many problems unresolved, but it is undeniable too that it contributed to economic stability and laid the foundations for current economic development.

There is a great deal of fluidity and activity at the regional level. Traditional integration schemes are in crisis or have gone through a process of reform to bring them in line with the new priorities of the social and economic agenda. New solutions have been suggested, such as the ALBA, which reflects the radical vision of its proponents, or UNASUR, which instead seems to reveal the prevailing pragmatism of its supporters. More may be in store if the project of a political Community of Latin American and Caribbean States (CELAC) materializes effectively and within a reasonable time. As in the past, the rhetoric of Latin American unity continues to coexist with political, economic and other divisions. Brazil's regional and international rise and the redefinition of the continent's relations with the United States will have decisive effects on the future of Latin American regionalism.

In international relations, Latin America has become more assertive and autonomous. Relations with the United States, aside from a few small rhetorical excesses, are still good and fundamental for the economy of most of the continent, which now seems able to negotiate on more favourable terms with its powerful neighbour. Cultural and historic ties with Europe have not translated into a similar strengthening of links with the European Union, which, although an important partner for Latin America, seems to be losing ground to the advantage of China. The Asian giant is the newest player, a source of opportunities but also potential challenges.

In summary, Latin America in the twenty-first century seems to have finally accepted the need to formulate and activate genuinely local solutions in response to its own needs and interests at the state, regional and global levels. Equally, the continent remains torn between three characteristic dilemmas: rhetoric versus pragmatism, unity versus diversity, and change versus continuity. In several cases, the suitable combination seems to have been found. Vitally, the future of the continent will depend on the quality of its ruling class. This is a key factor for the success of any community.

Notes

Introduction

1 Alain Rouquié (1998), *Amérique latine. Introduction à l'Extrême-Occident*, Seuil, Paris.

1 The states of Latin America

1 Geraldine Lievesley and Steve Ludlam (2009), *Reclaiming Latin America. Experiments in Radical Social Democracy*, Zed Books, London.

2 Thomas E. Skidmore (1999), *Brazil. Five Centuries of Change*, Oxford University Press, Oxford and New York, p. 225.

3 Ibid.

4 Findings quoted in *The Economist* (2008), 'Half the nation, a hundred million citizens strong', 11 September.

5 Alfred P. Montero (2006), *Brazilian Politics*, Polity Press, Cambridge.

6 Edwin Williamson (1992), *The Penguin History of Latin America*, Penguin Books, London, p. 480.

7 Jonathan C. Brown (2004), *A Brief History of Argentina*, Facts on File, New York, pp. 250–72.

8 Ibid.

9 José Natanson (2007), 'Pobreza y crecimineto en América Latina – diálogo con Bernardo Kiksberg', *Safe Democracy*, 16 November 2007.

10 *The Economist* (2006), 'Tucking in to the good times', 19 November.

11 *Oxford Analytica* (2011), 'Argentina: robust GDP growth will slow this year', 21 January.

12 Christopher Wylde (2010), 'Argentina, Kirchnerismo and Neo-desarrollismo. Argentine political economy under the administration of Nestor Kirchner 2003–2007', FLACSO working document no. 14, Buenos Aires, April.

13 Klaus Schmidt-Hebbels (2006), 'Chile's economic growth', *Cuadernos de Economía*, 43, May, pp. 5–48.

14 J. Samuel Valenzuela and Arturo Valenzuela (2005), 'Chile: the development, breakdown, and recovery of democracy', in J. Knippers Black, *Latin America: Its Problems and Its Promise*, Westview Press, Boulder (CO), p. 534.

15 Ibid., p. 538.

16 Ignacio Ramonet (2007), 'Hugo Chávez', *Le Monde Diplomatique*, August.

17 As quoted in *The Economist* (2007), 'The wind goes out of the revolution', 6 December.

18 Ibid.

19 All findings and figures as quoted in Ricardo Angoso (2007), 'Analizando el proceso revolucionario venezolano', *Safe Democracy*, 3 December.

20 John Crabtree and Laurence Whitehead (eds) (2008), *Bolivia. Unresolved tensions. Past and*

present, University of Pittsburgh Press, Pittsburgh, part I, pp. 9–60.

21 Reprimarization refers to the return of Latin American economies to high reliance on the export of primary goods such as minerals, hydrocarbons, metals, agricultural produce and unprocessed foodstuffs.

2 Latin American regionalism

1 Andrew Hurrell (1995), 'Regionalism in theoretical perspective', in L. Fawcett and A. Hurrell, *Regionalism in World Politics*, Oxford University Press, Oxford, pp. 37–73.

2 Raúl Prebisch (1950), *The Economic Development of Latin America and Its Principal Problems*, United Nations, New York.

3 John Williamson (1997), 'The Washington Consensus revisited', in Louis Emmerij (ed.), *Economic and Social Development into the XXI Century*, Inter-American Development Bank, Washington, DC, pp. 48–61.

4 David Held and Anthony McGrew (2003), *The Global Transformations Reader*, Polity Press, Cambridge.

5 Gian Luca Gardini (2010), *The Origins of MERCOSUR*, Palgrave, New York.

6 Ibid.

7 Karl Kaltenthaler and Frank O. Mora (2002), 'Explaining Latin American integration: the case of MERCOSUR', *Review of International Political Economy*, 9(1): 72–97.

8 Barry Buzan (2011), 'A world order without superpowers: decentred globalism', *International Relations*, 25(1): 3–25.

3 Latin America in the world

1 John Williamson (1990), *Latin American Adjustment: How Much Has Happened?*, Institute for International Economics, Washington, DC.

2 Peter Hakim (2006), 'Is Washington losing Latin America?', *Foreign Affairs*, January/February.

3 James Petras (2006), 'US–Latin American relations: ruptures, reaction and the illusion of times past', *Dissent Voice*, 2 November.

4 Larry Birns (2007), 'Less of the same: lackluster US–Latin American relations to continue under second Bush administration', *COHA Papers*, 21 February.

5 Petras (2006).

6 Miguel Angel Centeno (2008), 'Left behind? Latin America in a globalized world', *The American Interest*, January/February.

7 Stephen Johnson (2005), 'US diplomacy towards Latin America: a legacy of uneven engagement', Heritage Lecture no. 895, Heritage Foundation, 23 August.

8 The World Bank (2011), online database, data.worldbank.org/.

9 Centeno (2008).

10 Petras (2006).

11 European Commission (2006), *The European Union, Latin America and the Caribbean: A Strategic Partnership*, Office for Official Publications of the European Communities, Luxembourg.

12 Eurostat (2011), *Latin America–EU: Indicators, trade and investment*, epp.eurostat.ec.europa.eu/statistics_explained/index.php/Latin_America-EU_-_economic_indicators,_trade_and_investment.

13 European Commission (2007), *Latin America: Regional Programming Document 2007–2013*, 12 July 2007 (E/2007/1417).

14 European Commission (2009), *EU–Latin America: Global Players in Partnership*, Brussels, 30 September 2009 (COM(2009) 495/3).

15 European Commission DG Trade (2011), *Bilateral Relations: Countries and regions*, ec.europa.eu/trade/creating-opportunities/bilateral-relations/countries-and-regions/.

16 Ali El Agraa (2003), 'EU/Latin American relationship: with emphasis on Mercosur', Paper 37, Japan Society of Social Science on Latin America, July.

17 European Commission DG Trade (2011).

18 Ibid.

19 Economic Commission for Latin America and the Caribbean (2010), *The People's Republic of China and Latin America and the Caribbean: Towards a strategic relationship*, United Nations, Santiago.

Bibliography

General works

Meade, T. A. (2010) *A History of Modern Latin America, 1800 to the present*, Chichester: Wiley-Blackwell, provides a complete summary of Latin American history since independence with a final chapter dedicated to twenty-first-century Latin America.

Panizza, F. (2009) *Contemporary Latin America. Development and Democracy beyond the Washington Consensus*, London: Zed Books, offers an accessible and insightful overview of the last twenty-five years of Latin American history.

Reid, M. (2007) *Forgotten Continent. The Battle for Latin America's Soul*, London/New Haven, CT: Yale University Press, is the best attempt to explore the transition from neoliberal regimes to those of the pink tide from a historical and economic point of view.

Williamson, E. (1992) *The Penguin History of Latin America*, London: Penguin, is still very valid although a little dated.

Recent history and individual countries

Lievesley, G. and S. Ludlam (2009) *Reclaiming Latin America. Experiments in Radical Social Democracy*, London: Zed Books, provides a clear analysis of the new progressive governments.

Reid, M. (2007) *Forgotten Continent*, mentioned above, is also useful.

Santiso, J. (2006) *Latin America's Political Economy of the Possible*, Cambridge, MA: MIT Press, describes how institutions and policies are connected to social reality from a political economy perspective.

Argentina

Lewis, C. (2002) *Argentina. A Short History*, Oxford: Oneworld.

Romero, L. A. (2002) *A History of Argentina in the Twentieth Century*, Pittsburgh, PA: Penn State University Press.

Hedges, J. (2011) *Argentina: A Modern History*, London: I.B.Tauris.

Brazil

Montero, A. (2005) *Brazilian Politics*, Cambridge: Polity Press.

Roett, R. (2010) *The New Brazil*, Washington, DC: Brookings Institution.

Skidmore, T. E. (1999) *Brazil: Five Centuries of Change*, Oxford: Oxford University Press.

Vidal Luna, F. and H. S. Klein (2006) *Brazil since 1980*, Cambridge: Cambridge University Press.

Chile

Collier, S. and W. Sater (2004) *A History of Chile, 1808–2002*, Cambridge: Cambridge University Press.

Huneeus, C. (2007) *The Pinochet Regime*, Boulder, CO: Lynne Rienner.

Bolivia

Crabtree, J. and L. Whitehead (eds) (2008) *Bolivia. Unresolved Tensions. Past and Present*, Pittsburgh, PA: University of Pittsburgh Press.

Klein, H. S. (2003) *A Concise History of Bolivia*, Cambridge: Cambridge University Press.

Venezuela

Gott, R. (2005) *Hugo Chávez and the Bolivarian Revolution*, London: Verso.

Wilpert, G. (2007) *Changing Venezuela by Taking Power*, London: Verso.

Summary of the recent history of Latin America

Knippers Black, J. (2005) *Latin America: Its Problems and Its Promise*, Boulder, CO: Westview Press.

Latin American regionalism

Dabene, O. (2009) *The Politics of Regional Integration in Latin America*, New York: Palgrave Macmillan, offers an updated overview of the key themes and projects of Latin American regionalism.

Fawcett, L. and A. Hurrell (eds) (1995) *Regionalism in World Politics*, Oxford: Oxford University Press, is a vital work for its theory and empirical content.

Mace, G. and L. Bélanger (1999) *The Americas in Transition. The Contours of Regionalism*, Boulder, CO/London: Lynne Rienner, is an excellent but slightly dated work that concentrates on the 1990s.

Mercosur

Dominguez, F. and M. Guedes de Oliveira (eds) (2004) *Mercosur between Integration and Democracy*, New York/Oxford: Peter Lang, analyses Mercosur as a product of globalization.

Gardini, G. L. (2010) *The Origins of Mercosur*, New York: Palgrave Macmillan, explores the roots and formation of Mercosur.

NAFTA

Coffey, P. (1999) *NAFTA. Past, Present and Future*, Boston, MA/London: Kluwer Academic, is a good introduction to the first years of NAFTA.

Developments in the twenty-first century

Gardini, G. L. (2011) 'Unity and diversity in Latin American visions of regional integration', in G. L. Gardini and P. W. Lambert (eds), *Latin American Foreign Policies. Between Ideology and Pragmatism*, New York: Palgrave Macmillan, pp. 235–54, dissects and compares Mercosur, Alba and Unasur.

The inter-American system

Domínguez, J. I. (2000) *The Future of Inter-American Relations*, London: Routledge, offers an interesting overview and reflection.

The international relations of Latin America

Buzan, B. (2011) 'A world order without superpowers: decentred globalism', *International Relations*, 25(1): 3–25.

Gardini, G. L. and P. W. Lambert (eds) (2011) *Latin American Foreign Policies. Between Ideology and Pragmatism*, New York: Palgrave Macmillan, analyses the last twenty years of foreign policy of eleven countries and three regional projects.

Pope Atkins, G. (1999) *Latin America and the Caribbean in the International System*, Boulder, CO: Westview Press, is a bit outdated but still deals with the structural factors of Latin America's position in the international context.

US–Latin America relations

Birns, L. (2007) 'Less of the same: lackluster US–Latin American relations to continue under second Bush administration', *COHA Papers*, 21 February.

Bulmer-Thomas, V. and J. Dunkerley (eds) (1999) *The United States and Latin America: The New Agenda*, London: ILAS.

Crandall, R. (2008) *The United States and Latin America after the Cold War*, Cambridge: Cambridge University Press.

Hakim, P. (2006) 'Is Washington losing Latin America?', *Foreign Affairs*, January/February.

Petras, J. (2006) 'US–Latin American relations: ruptures, reaction and the illusion of times past', *Dissent Voice*, 2 November.

Smith, P. (2000) *Talons of the Eagle*, Oxford: Oxford University Press.

EU–Latin American relations

El Agraa, A. (2003) *EU/Latin American Relationship: With Emphasis on Mercosur*, Paper 37, Japan Society of Social Science on Latin America, July.

European Commission (2006) *The European Union, Latin America and the Caribbean: A Strategic Partnership*, Luxembourg: Office for Official Publications of the European Communities.

Jaguaribe, H. and A. Vasconcelos (2003) *The European Union, Mercosur and the New World Order*, London: Frank Cass.

Sanahuja, J. A. (2008) 'The European Union and Latin America: the common agenda after the Lima Summit', ICEI Paper 07, July. Many more interesting works by this leading scholar in the field are available in Spanish.

China and Latin America

Devlin, R., A. Estevadeordal and A. Rodríguez (2006) *The Emergence of China. Opportunities and Challenges for Latin America and the Caribbean*, Cambridge, MA: Harvard University Press.

Evan Ellis, R. (2009) *China in Latin America*, Boulder, CO: Lynne Rienner.

Hearn, A. H. and J. L. Leon-Manriquez (eds) (2011) *China Engages Latin America*, Boulder, CO: Lynne Rienner.

Globalization and Latin America

Centeno, M. A. (2008) 'Left behind? Latin America in a globalized world', *The American Interest*, January/February.

Websites

The following websites provide useful and precise updates on Latin American current affairs.

www.eclac.org (the webpage of the UN Economic Commission

for Latin America and the Caribbean)
www.celare.org (on EU–Latin American relations)
www.english.safe-democracy.org (Safe Democracy provides a Latin American view of Latin America)
www.clarin.com (the biggest Argentinian daily newspaper)
www.folha.uol.com.br (an influential Brazilian daily, based in São Paolo)
www.coha.org (Council of Hemispheric Affairs think tank)
www.economist.com (British magazine which specializes in international affairs)
www.nytimes.com (the daily paper the *New York Times* with an excellent international section)
www.bbc.co.uk (with regular updates from around the world)
petras.lahaine.org/index.php (for a critical but informed view of Latin America and international affairs)
www.mercosur.int; www.comunidadandina.org
www.sica.org

Index